The Chorus in Opera

A Guide to the Repertory

by
David P. DeVenney
and
Craig R. Johnson

The Scarecrow Press, Inc.
Metuchen, N.J., & London
1993

British Library Cataloguing-in-Publication data available

Library of Congress Cataloging-in-Publication Data

DeVenney, David P., 1958-
    The chorus in opera : a guide to the repertory / by David P.
  DeVenney and Craig R. Johnson.
       p.   cm.
    Includes indexes.
    ISBN 0-8108-2620-8
    1. Choral music--Bibliography.   2. Opera--Bibliography.
  I. Johnson, Craig R.   II. Title.
  ML128.C48D47 1993
  782.1--dc20   92-33252

To Cass, Elizabeth, and Maria

Table of Contents

Preface

The concept of a "standard" choral repertory has undergone significant changes over the past twenty years. Recently, ensembles and conductors have increasingly looked to non-traditional sources for expanding the literature that they perform. Those sources include the art music and rich folk traditions of Scandinavia, Asia and Eastern Europe, and choral literature based on the music of Africans and Native Americans. Recent conventions of the American Choral Directors Association have confirmed and helped proliferate this trend.

Singers and orchestras have often mined the rich field of opera in search of music for study and performance. While choral excerpts from opera are also performed, those performances have been infrequent, and often limited to a relatively few choruses widely known, such as "Va pensiero" from Verdi's *Nabucco*, or the spinning chorus from Wagner's *Der fliegende Holländer*.

The purpose of this volume is therefore two-fold: to aid choral conductors in search of new and interesting literature, and to investigate the choral resources of opera in the same manner that it has been searched for solo vocal and instrumental repertory. Our goal in compiling this volume has been primarily to add to the body of choral repertory, and not necessarily to annotate opera scenes that make extensive use of chorus. Indeed, the reader will often *not* find within this volume some of the most famous choral and ensemble passages from opera.

For example, Act II of Puccini's *La Bohème* is famous for its use of large choral forces. While the chorus is onstage throughout this act, the scene is dramatically and musically dependent upon the solo voices. Only a small choral portion near the end of the act is excerptable according to our guidelines. Similarly, *La Wally* by Alfredo Catalani contains a scene in Act III where the chorus rushes to the aid of Wally as she tries to rescue Hagenbach, who has fallen into a deep crevice. While the chorus sings frequently, the text consists primarily of outcries of concern ("What's going on?" and "Look what has happened!"). These choral outbursts are widely separated by orchestral interludes and phrases sung by solo characters. As such, the choral portion of this scene makes little sense out of context and it was not included here.

In Cilea's *Adriana Lecouvreur* the chorus is often onstage during Act III, especially during the party scene and the ballet which follows. The longest choral phrase, however, is only eight measures long, and hence not considered excerptable. A jazz trio opens Bernstein's *Trouble in Tahiti*. While it might be used with a small vocal jazz ensemble, it was written for solo voices. A choral performance would violate the composer's intentions, and so this and similar scenes were not excerpted either.

These few examples serve in a general way to illustrate our thinking. The reader will find further information on the criteria for inclusion of excerpts in the Guide to Use that follows this Preface.

Exceptions aside, there is a wealth of new repertory in this volume. The user will find works to fit virtually any choral force – children's voices, men's or women's voices, mixed ensembles in single or double choir, either four-part or divided choir – as well as works of virtually any duration, and for almost any occasion. The user will also find choruses written for all ability levels, and each excerpt is rated from "easy" to "difficult." These categories are more fully described in the Guide to Use.

Several text types emerged among the various choruses. Wedding choruses, hunting choruses, drinking or party choruses, and laudatory choruses (to a lord of the manor or other such luminary) are among the most frequent, which may not be surprising. These are also among the most performable excerpts included here. There are many other choruses which do not fall into these genre categories that are also worth exploring, such as the disturbing "Quel plaisir! quelle joie" from Act V of Halévy's *La Juive* or the festive, exuberant "Sing Hubbard" from *Regina* by Marc Blitzstein.

There are choruses annotated here that are familiar to opera goers and choral conductors (such as the Verdi and Wagner examples described above), and many more that will be new. There are choruses taken from opera's early days, from such works as Monteverdi's *Orfeo*; and those of relatively recent vintage, such as the difficult but delightful dinner chorus from Britten's *Death in Venice*.

In short, *The Chorus in Opera* puts into the user's hands a quick, readable guide to an exciting new wealth of choral literature culled from the field of opera, which has proved such fertile ground for concert literature in the past. We hope that conductors seeking new repertory, musicologists exploring the role of the chorus in opera throughout its history, and the professional or amateur choral or opera enthusiast will find within these covers, and among these nearly six hundred choruses, many hours of happy and fruitful browsing.

* * * * *

We wish to gratefully acknowledge the many people and groups who have helped us compile this volume, first among them the Humanities Advisory Committee at Otterbein College who granted funds which enabled us to travel to New York and Washington in pursuit of scores and other materials. Dr. Ralph Pearson, Vice President for Academic Affairs, and the Otterbein College Sabbatical Leaves Committee provided Dr. Johnson with leave time to complete his portion of this volume. Mary Ellen Armentrout, research librarian of the Courtwright Memorial Library at Otterbein, was extremely efficient and helpful with our many Inter-Library Loan requests. Eero Richmond and the staff of the American Music Center in New York were generous with their time and patience, as was the staff of the Music and Dance Library of The Ohio State University, where the bulk of the research was completed. We also extend appreciation to our student assistant Stephen B. Lantis, who diligently searched publishers' catalogs for editions of these operas.

Finally, we would like to thank our families and friends, whose patience and support allowed us to complete this volume in a timely fashion.

Guide to Use

Background

The Catalog of Works lists choruses which have been excerpted from standard operatic repertory from the Baroque period through the present day. In order to determine standard repertory, we consulted one of the most widely respected guides to operatic literature, *Kobbé's Complete Opera Book*,[1] which lists over three hundred operas by 109 composers.

In some cases, operas included in *Kobbé's* had no excerptable choruses or used no chorus at all. In a few instances, we were not able to locate a particular score for perusal. There were also a few works which, in our opinion, belonged to the genre of oratorio rather than opera, confirmed in part by their Library of Congress categorization.[2] A list of these operas may be found in Appendix A. In all, however, the Catalog of Works contains annotations of nearly six hundred choruses from 218 operas by ninety composers.

---

[1] Harewood, Earl of, ed. *Kobbé's Complete Opera Book*. London: The Bodley Head, 1987.

[2] The Library of Congress assigns opera classification numbers from M1500 to M1508.

Criteria for Inclusion of Excerpts

To be included in the Catalog, choruses needed to have a clear beginning and ending, defined by appropriate harmonic cadences, with melodic and rhythmic conclusiveness. We also required the text of each chorus to be understandable out of context of the scene from which it was taken.

Some use of soloists has been permitted. However, those choruses which require more than two or three solo voices, or which have very difficult solo parts in terms of range or tessitura, have usually been excluded from the Catalog. There are a few excerpts included in the Catalog that require five or six solo voices whose lines are doubled in the choral parts. These choruses have been included, and the conductor may decide to use soloists or not. Choruses which function as musical underpinning for a predominantly solo scene were excluded, as was ensemble music, intended for a group of solo voices rather than choral forces.

Very short choral "outbursts" or those choruses which consist of several sections of only two to three phrases interspersed with much solo or orchestral writing have not been excerpted. In general, when we questioned whether or not a chorus was excerptable, we have erred on the side of exclusiveness.

Using the Catalog

The Catalog of Works is organized alphabetically by composer, and then alphabetically by title of opera. Where there are two or more excerptable choruses within an opera, they are listed chronologically (i.e., choruses from Act I before those from Act II, etc.).

Each excerpt in the Catalog of Works has a reference number. These reference numbers run consecutively throughout the

Catalog and in the indexes at the end of the book, they refer the reader to specific choruses. Each excerpt is annotated according to the following guidelines:

> Composer, *Opera* (Date of Composition)
> Librettist(s)
> Publisher(s)
> **XXX** 1. Act, Scene or Number, "Title of Scene or First Line of Text"
> 2. Performing forces needed
> 3. Duration
> 4. Difficulty level
> 5. Description of chorus
> N.B.: Unusual problems or concerns, or other information about the excerpt.

Titles of operas are given in the original language if they are in English, French, German, Italian, Latin, or Spanish. Other opera titles are listed first in their most common English translation, with their original title given secondarily. The only exceptions to this occur when the title of an opera is also a proper name, in which case the original language is used (e.g., Moussorgskii's *Ivan Susanin*, for which the title is the same in either transliterated Russian or in English). The title index is inclusive of all titles and translations.

The date of composition given is the final completion date of the opera, nearly always coinciding with its first performance. In some cases, when a work was substantially revised at a later date, that date is also given (e.g., Gounod's *Faust*, completed in 1859, but revised in 1869, is annotated with both dates).

When soloists are named in the excerpted scene, those names are listed along with their voice parts under annotation two. Users should assume that the excerpted chorus requires accompaniment unless the annotation states "unaccompanied."

Assuming that these works were written with mature voices in mind, we have categorized the choruses with good college or community choirs as the standard performing ensemble. The difficulty of choruses is rated as follows:

"Easy" - can be sung by good high school choirs and
other younger voices.

"Medium" - can be sung by average small college or
advanced high school choral ensembles with little
difficulty; few or no soloists are included in the
excerpt.

"Moderately Difficult" - requires strong choral singers
and more advanced musicianship; solo voices, if
required, must be of good quality.

"Difficult" - requires very strong choral singing and
solo voices of high quality and musicianship. These
choruses are intended for the most advanced
college, university, or community choirs.

The fifth part of the annotation gives a description of the chorus
(i.e., "funeral chorus," "chorus of peasants, knights, villagers," etc.),
often with a brief summary of the text or a short synopsis of the
scene from which the chorus is taken.

The question of editions of these operas is a difficult one to
address accurately. We have listed the publisher(s) of the edition
that we used to annotate the chorus, in addition to any editions we
could find in current publishers' catalogs.[3] Many works exist only
in nineteenth-century publications and are difficult to obtain. In
some instances we have cited a library location where a copy of the
vocal score is available. The user of this volume is encouraged to
locate hard-to-find scores through *The National Union Catalog*,
major research libraries, inter-library loan, and other such
resources. We have made no attempt to list separate octavo
publications of individual choruses. While some of the choruses
annotated here do exist in this form, their availability can be
readily ascertained through retail music dealers and through
current publishers' catalogs.

---

[3]Many catalogs list opera scores that are part of their stock, in addition to
those scores which they also publish. All operas found in these catalogs are listed
under "publishers."

There are six indexes to this volume: to titles of operas, to first lines and titles of scenes, and to librettists, as well as indexes to choral performing forces, to difficulty level of the excerpts, and to the duration of the excerpts.

Abbreviations Used

A	alto
AMC	American Music Center, New York City
B	bass
Bar	baritone
(cw)	"collected works" edition
dbl.	double
inst.	instrument(s)
LC	Library of Congress, Washington, DC
M	mezzo-soprano
mss.	manuscript(s)
n.d.	no date
ob.	oboe
opt.	optional
orch.	orchestra
OSU	Music/Dance Library, The Ohio State University, Columbus
pno.	piano
S	soprano
T	tenor
timp.	timpani
tpt.	trumpet
trbn.	trombone

Catalog of Works

A

Auber, Daniel François. *Fra Diavolo* (1830)
Librettist: Eugène Scribe
Publisher: Broude Bros., Kalmus, Novello, B. Schott's Söhne,
   G. Schirmer
1 1. Act I, No. 1, "En bons militaires buvons"
   2. TTBB; Lorenzo (T)
   3. 3.5 minutes
   4. Moderately Difficult
   5. The soldiers sing a drinking song before setting out
      the next day to catch the robber known as Fra
      Diavolo.

2 1. Act III, No. 13, "C'est grande fête"
   2. SATB; several incidental soli
   3. 3 minutes
   4. Medium
   5. A wedding processional, accompanying the unwilling
      Zerline who is being pressed to marry Francesco,
      a miller.

Auber, Daniel François. *La muette de Portici* (1828)
Librettist: Eugène Scribe
Publishers: Brandus, Broude Bros., Garland, Peters

3   1. Act I, No. 2, "Du prince objet de notre amour"
    2. STB divisi
    3. 3 minutes
    4. Medium
    5. The Neapolitans cheer Alfonso, the viceroy's son, on his way to wed Elvira, a Spanish princess.

4   1. Act I, No. 4b, "O Dieu puissant"
    2. STB divisi; Selva (Bar)
    3. 4 minutes
    4. Medium
    5. A festive choral prayer as Alfonso and Elvira celebrate their marriage.

5   1. Act III, No. 6, "Amis, amis"
    2. STB divisi
    3. 4.5 minutes
    4. Medium
    5. A chorus of fishermen, casting their nets, greets the morning.

6   1. Act III, No. 7, "Barcarolle"
    2. STB divisi; Masaniello (T), Borella (Bar)
    3. 5 minutes
    4. Moderately Difficult
    5. Masaniello, Fenella's brother, mourns his sister's disappearance before bursting into a barcarolle which galvanizes the fishermen's hostility towards their Spanish oppressors.

7   1. Act III, No. 11, "Choeur du marché"
    2. STB divisi
    3. 6 minutes
    4. Medium

      5. The crowd in the marketplace beckons "young and
         old, large and small" to come and buy their wares.

8   1. Act III, Finale, "Prière"
       2. STB divisi
       3. 3.5 minutes
       4. Moderately Difficult
       5. A prayer ("Heavenly Father, have mercy") after
         Selva is slain by Masaniello.
       N.B. There are solo lines for Masaniello, Pietro, and
       Borella (TBB), but they are doubled by the chorus
       throughout and the parts may be dispensed with in
       performance if desired.

B

Balfe, Michael William. *The Bohemian Girl* (1843)
Librettist: Alfred Bunn
Publisher: G. Schirmer
9   1. Act I, Scene 1, "Up with the banner"
       2. STB
       3. 3 minutes
       4. Easy
       5. A patriotic chorus, praising the Austrian flag.

10   1. Act I, Scene 1, "In the gypsy's life"
       2. SATB
       3. 4 minutes
       4. Moderately Difficult
       5. A chorus of gypsies sings of the attractions of their
         way of life.

11   1. Act I, Finale, "Follow, follow with heart and arm"
       2. SATB divisi
       3. 2.5 minutes

4. Medium
5. The conclusion of the Finale, where the gentry and soldiers are seen chasing around the stage in search of Devilshoof, who has fled and blocked the way.

Beethoven, Ludwig van. *Fidelio* (1805)
Librettists: Joseph Sonnleithner and Friedrich Treitschke, after J.W. Bouilly
Publishers: Bärenreiter (cw), Boosey and Hawkes, Broude Bros., Eulenberg, Dover, Jerona, Kalmus, G. Schirmer
12   1. Act I, Scene 9, "O welche Lust, in freier Luft"
      2. TTBB; short T, Bar soli
      3. 7 minutes
      4. Difficult
      5. The prisoners temporarily gain their freedom, after Leonore persuades Rocco to let them walk in the garden.

13   1. Act II, Scene 7, "Heil sei dem Tag"
      2. SATB/TB dbl. choir
      3. 5 minutes
      4. Difficult
      5. The townspeople and prisoners hail Don Fernando, the Prime Minister, when he arrives at the prison to right the wrongs of tyranny, prior to the release of Florestan.

Bellini, Vincenzo. *Beatrice di Tenda* (1833)
Librettist: Felice Romani
Publishers: Broude Bros., Garland, Kalmus, G. Schirmer
14   1. Act I, No. 2, "Tu, signor"
      2. SATB; Filippo (Bar)
      3. 4.5 minutes
      4. Medium

5. In the courtyard of the palace of Filippo, Duke of Milan, his courtiers react with concern when the Duke explains that he is tired of his wife, Beatrice, and yearns for the love of Agnese.

15
1. Act I, No. 6, "Come, ah come"
2. SSA
3. 3.5 minutes
4. Medium
5. This short, lyrical chorus is sung by Beatrice's ladies-in-waiting, commiserating with her about her husband's spurning of her love.

16
1. Act I, No. 9, "Lo, vestale"
2. TB
3. 5 minutes
4. Medium
5. Armed soldiers discuss the erratic and mysterious behavior of the Duke, and conclude that events will soon show his hand.

17
1. Act II, No. 13, "Lasso! e può il ciel"
2. STB
3. 5 minutes
4. Moderately Difficult
5. At a tribunal in the castle the chorus announces that Orombello, who had been caught earlier offering aid to Beatrice, has confessed to his crime under torture.

18
1. Act II, No. 16, "Ah! non sia la misera"
2. SSAA
3. 3 minutes
4. Moderately Difficult
5. Beatrice's ladies-in-waiting pray at her cell, as she awaits her sentence of beheading.

Bellini, Vincenzo. *I Capuletti ed i Montecchi* (1830)
Librettist: Felice Romani
Publishers: Broude Bros., Garland, Kalmus, G. Schirmer
19   1. Act I, Scene 1, "Aggiorna appena"
     2. SATB
     3. 4 minutes
     4. Moderately Difficult
     5. The Capulets' followers have gathered in the
       palace, wondering if they are threatened
       by the feud their leaders have with the Montagues.

20   1. Act I, Scene 8, "Lieta notte"
     2. TTBB
     3. 3 minutes
     4. Moderately Difficult
     5. A short chorus, sung by the Capulets in the
       courtyard of their palace. The wedding festivities
       have begun and this spirited chorus remarks on
       the enjoyment ahead for the young couple.

Bellini, Vincenzo. *Norma* (1831)
Librettist: Felice Romani
Publishers: Broude Bros., Garland, Kalmus, Ricordi, G.
  Schirmer
21   1. Act I, Scene 1, "Dell'aura tua profetica"
     2. TBB; Oroveso (B)
     3. 6 minutes
     4. Medium
     5. Druids and warriors invoke the aid and protection
       of the god Irminsul to help them destroy the
       Roman legions and drive them from Gaul.
     N.B. The part for Oroveso may be omitted, as it is
     usually doubled by the chorus basses. A short section
     for solo voices may also be sung tutti.

22   1. Act I, Scene 3, "Norma viene: le cinge la chioma"
     2. STB divisi

3. 3.5 minutes
4. Medium
5. Accompanied by virgins and priestesses, the Druids
   and warriors assemble in a grove and sing a chorus
   acclaiming Norma and invoking the protection of
   the god Irminsul for their war efforts.

23 1. Act II, Scene 4, "Non parti?"
  2. TBB divisi
  3. 7 minutes
  4. Medium
  5. A "conference" chorus between the Gallic warriors
   and the Druids, where they report on the
   movements of the Romans. In the end, the two
   factions delay attacking until they can do so at full
   strength.

24 1. Act II, Scene 6, "Guerra, guerra!"
  2. SATB; Norma (S), Oroveso (B)
  3. 3 minutes
  4. Moderately Difficult
  5. Norma has struck the shield three times, signalling
   for war; the people answer in a fiery chorus in
   which they swear to wipe the Romans from the
   face of the earth.

Bellini, Vincenzo. *Il Pirata* (1827)
Librettist: Felice Romani, after Rev. R.C. Maturin
Publishers: Broude Bros., Garland, Kalmus, Ricordi, G.
 Schirmer
25 1. Act I, Scene 1, "Ciel! qual procella orribile"
  2. SATB; Solitario (Bar)
  3. 7 minutes
  4. Moderately Difficult
  5. The villagers and fishermen watch in anguish the
   shipwreck of Gualtiero and the pirates he
   commands in this agitated, driven chorus.

N.B. Solitario's part is nearly always doubled in the choral parts.

26   1. Act I, Scene 5, "Viva! viva!"
      2. TTBB; Itulbo (T)
      3. 6.5 minutes
      4. Moderately Difficult
      5. A rousing chorus of pirates, drinking on the castle terrace; they are warned by Itulbo not to give away their identities as pirates.

27   1. Act I, Scene 7, "Più temuto, più splendido nome"
      2. TTBB divisi
      3. 5.5 minutes
      4. Moderately Difficult
      5. A chorus of the Duke's soldiers celebrates victory over the pirates.
      N.B. The scene may be lengthened by the addition of the following aria and chorus for Ernesto (Bar), the Duke of Caldora.

28   1. Act II, Scene 1, "Che rechi tu?"
      2. SSA; Adele (S)
      3. 4 minutes
      4. Moderately Difficult
      5. Adele, Imogene's companion, talks to her ladies-in-waiting, assuring them of Imogene's good health.
      N.B. Much of Adele's music is doubled by the choral parts.

29   1. Act II, Scene 8, "Lasso! perir così"
      2. SATB
      3. 4.5 minutes
      4. Moderately Difficult
      5. The warriors and ladies of the court gather in the great hall of the castle to mourn the Duke's death and swear to avenge his murder.

Bellini, Vincenzo. *I Puritani* (1855)
Librettist: Count Pepoli
Publishers: Broude Bros., Garland, Kalmus, Ricordi, G.
  Schirmer

30 1. Act I, No. 1, "All'erta" and "Quando la tromba
          squilla"
       2. TTBB
       3. 4.5 minutes
       4. Medium
       5. Bruno and a company of Cromwell's soldiers stir
          into activity as a trumpet sounds, answering a call
          to battle where they say they will annihilate their
          enemies, the Stuarts. The chorus begins rather
          quietly and climaxes with repeated cries of
          "Death!"

31 1. Act I, No. 3, "A festa!"
       2. SATB
       3. 3 minutes
       4. Moderately Difficult
       5. The previous dark mood of the scene abruptly shifts
          as peasants crowd onstage, singing this brief,
          happy chorus of celebration for Elvira on her
          bridal day.

32 1. Act I, No. 6, "Ad Arturo honore"
       2. SATB
       3. 3 minutes
       4. Moderately Difficult
       5. The gathered lords and ladies of the castle, with the
          peasants, salute Arturo as he accepts their gifts on
          his wedding day. A majestic, stately chorus.

33 1. Act I, No. 12, "Ahi! dura scigura"
       2. SATB
       3. 7.5 minutes
       4. Difficult

5. Arturo has escaped, leaving Elvira behind. In this rousing Finale to Act I, the chorus calls down maledictions on Arturo's head.

N.B. The excerpt calls for several solo voices, all doubled in the choral parts.

34
1. Act II, No. 13, "Ahi! dolor"
2. SATB divisi
3. 8 minutes
4. Moderately Difficult
5. The villagers and Puritans bewail Elvira's loss, commenting that in her present madness she will surely die of unrequited love.

Bellini, Vincenzo. *La Sonnambula* (1834)
Librettist: Felice Romani
Publishers: Broude Bros., Kalmus, Ricordi, G. Schirmer

35
1. Act I, Scene 1, "Viva Amina!"
2. SATB
3. 2 minutes
4. Medium
5. A short, festive chorus sung by the villagers, in honor of Amina's wedding to Elvino, a well-to-do young farmer.

N.B. The scene may be significantly extended by the addition of the following cavatina for Lisa (S), which uses the same chorus material as Scene 1.

36
1. Act I, Scene 1, "In Elvezia non v'ha rosa"
2. SATB divisi; Lisa (S), Alessio (Bar)
3. 4 minutes
4. Moderately Difficult
5. Alessio, a young rustic, praises the beauty of Amina, much to Lisa's chagrin, who is a rival to Amina. The chorus echoes Alessio's sentiments, saying Amina's beauty shames the flowers and the stars.

37   1. Act II, Scene 1, "Qui la selva è più folta ed
              ombrosa"
           2. SATB
           3. 4.5 minutes
           4. Moderately Difficult
           5. A crowd of peasants travels to enlist the count's aid
              in clearing Amina's name; she has been accused of
              sleeping with the count. Along the way, they rest
              in a shady place and discuss how they will plead
              their case.

Bellini, Vincenzo. *La Straniera* (1829)
Librettist: Felice Romani
Publishers: Broude Bros., Garland, Kalmus, Ricordi, G.
  Schirmer

38   1. Act I, Scene 1, "Voga, voga"
           2. SATB
           3. 5 minutes
           4. Medium
           5. A group of peasants, in this pastoral chorus, hails
              the approaching wedding of Isoletta and
              Valdeburgo.

39   1. Act I, Scene 3, "Campo ai veltri"
           2. TB divisi; Osburgo (T)
           3. 3.5 minutes
           4. Medium
           5. At a clearing in the forest, Osburgo and his party
              sing a hunting chorus. In two parts, the second
              requires more range and dynamic control than the
              first.

40   1. Act II, Scene 3, "È dolce la vergine"
           2. SATB
           3. 4.5 minutes
           4. Medium
           5. A stately wedding hymn to Isoletta and Arturo.

41   1. Act II, Finale, "Pari all'amor degli angioli"
          2. SATB divisi; Alaide (S)
          3. 4 minutes
          4. Moderately Difficult
          5. The Prior announces that Alaide is really the Queen
             of Brittany. Arturo, in disbelief, plunges his sword
             into his own body. The chorus comments on the
             tragic scene, while Alaide laments the turn of fate
             that propels her to the throne at the expense of
             her happiness.
          N.B. The scene may be extended with the addition of
          the final chorus of grief and compassion, "Al ciel, lo
          spirto l'abbandona," which calls for several soloists.

Benedict, Julius. *The Lily of Kilarney* (1862)
Librettists: Dion Boucicault and John Oxenford
Publisher: Boosey and Hawkes

42   1. Act I, No. 1, "Another cheer"
          2. SATB
          3. 3 minutes
          4. Easy
          5. A party is underway and the assembled guests drink
             a toast to their host.

43   1. Act II, No. 8, "Tally-ho!"
          2. TTBB
          3. 3.5 minutes
          4. Medium
          5. A rousing hunting chorus, full of boisterous shouts
             of "Tally-ho!" The men hope to forget their
             problems in love by a morning of hunting.

44   1. Act III, No. 19, "The wedding day has come at last"
          2. SATB; Ann (S), Mrs. Cregan (M), Fr. Tom (Bar)
          3. 6 minutes
          4. Medium
          5. A wedding chorus of endless joy and happiness.

Berlioz, Hector. *Béatrice et Bénédict* (1862)
Librettist: composer, after William Shakespeare
Publishers: Bärenreiter, Broude Bros., Kalmus, G. Schirmer

45   1. Act I, No. 1, "Le More est en fuite"
     2. SATB
     3. 3.5 minutes
     4. Moderately Difficult
     5. A general chorus of rejoicing by the townspeople
       that they are no longer in danger from the Moors,
       who had besieged them.

46   1. Act I, No. 6, "Mourez, tendres époux"
     2. SATB
     3. 3 minutes
     4. Medium
     5. A "motet," rehearsed in the opera by Somarone, a
       conductor; in essence, a choral fugue on the
       wonders of love.
    N.B. The chorus is repeated later in this act.

47   1. Act III, No. 9, "Le vin de Syracuse"
     2. SATB; Somarone (B)
     3. 4 minutes
     4. Medium
     5. Led by Somarone, the chorus intones a lively
       drinking song.

48   1. Act II, No. 12, "Viens! viens, de l'hyménée"
     2. SAT; guitar
     3. 2.5 minutes
     4. Medium
     5. A paean to love, sung offstage.

49   1. Act II, No. 13, "Marche nuptiale"
     2. SATB; Beatrice (S), Ursula (A), Benedict (T), Don
       Pedro (B)
     3. 6 minutes
     4. Moderately Difficult

5. A wedding march, calling upon God to bless the
   forthcoming nuptials.
N.B. While much of the solo music is doubled in the
choral parts, there are contrasting lines that must be
performed.

Berlioz, Hector. *Benvenuto Cellini* (1838)
Librettists: Jules Barbier and du Wailly
Publishers: Broude Bros., Kalmus, G. Schirmer
50   1. Act II, No. 6, "À boire, à boire"
         2. TTBB; Ascanio (M), Cellini (T), Francesco (T),
            Bernardino (B)
         3. 12 minutes
         4. Difficult
         5. This delightful chorus follows Cellini's *romance*,
            in which he sings that love is more important than
            fame.
         N.B. Much of the solo music is doubled in the choral
         parts, although there are a number of important solo
         lines which must be sung.

51   1. Act II, Finale, "Venez, venez peuple de Rome"
         2. TB/SATB dbl. choir
         3. 14 minutes
         4. Difficult
         5. The first choral portion from the famous Carnival
            scene: a gay, festive chorus of maskers on the
            Piazza di Colonna.

Berlioz, Hector. *La Damnation de Faust* (1846)
Librettist: composer, after Johann W. von Goethe
Publishers: Bärenreiter (cw), Broude Bros., Editions Costallat,
   Eulenberg, Kalmus, B. Schott's Söhne, G. Schirmer
52   1. Act II, Scene 4, "Chant de la Fête de Paquis"
         2. SATB divisi; Faust (T)
         3. 7 minutes

4. Moderately Difficult
5. Faust encounters a group of townspeople celebrating Easter day with a processional; while they sing "Hosanna," he revels in the glories of spring.

53   1. Act II, Scene 6, "Choeur de Buveurs"
2. TTBB
3. 3.5 minutes
4. Medium
5. A drinking chorus.

54   1. Act II, Scene 6, "Amen"
2. TTBB
3. 2 minutes
4. Moderately Difficult
5. The drinkers add a rousing fugal "Amen" to a song sung by the barkeeper.

55   1. Act II, Scene 8, "Finale"
2. TTBB divisi; Faust (T), Méphistophélès (Bar)
3. 10 minutes
4. Difficult
5. Two choruses, one of soldiers and the other of students, join forces. The soldiers sing, "how ever grand the pain, the price is even grander," while the students and the principals (in Latin) sing of fleeting life.
N.B. Faust's and Méphistophélè's parts are usually doubled in the chorus and could be deleted.

56   1. Act IV, Scene 19, "Pandoemonium"
2. TTBB
3. 4.5 minutes
4. Difficult
5. A choir of demons in Hell, in "enchanting" (nonsense) syllables, sings a furious, hair-raising chorus.

57   1. Epilogue, "Sur la terre"
       2. SATB divisi; S solo
       3. 5 minutes
       4. Moderately Difficult
       5. The apotheosis of Marguerite. A heavenly chorus
          calls her to come.

Berlioz, Hector. *Les Troyens* (1863)
Librettist: composer, after Vergil
Publishers: Bärenreiter (cw), Broude Bros., Editions
    Choudens, Eulenberg, Kalmus, G. Schirmer
58   1. Act I, Scene 1-2, "De Carthage les crieux"
       2. SATB
       3. 8 minutes
       4. Moderately Difficult
       5. At the abandoned camp of the Greeks, the people
          rejoice that their ten years of captivity are over.

59   1. Act III, Scene 2, "Chaque jour voit grandir la colère
          des dieux!"
       2. TTB; Panthée (B)
       3. 6.5 minutes
       4. Moderately Difficult
       5. A chorus of "invisible men" converges with the
          Trojan chiefs in a forest.

60   1. Act V, Finale, "Haine éternelle à la race d'Enée"
       2. SATB
       3. 4 minutes
       4. Medium
       5. As Dido dies, a vision of Rome, the eternal city,
          rises behind her pyre; the chorus sings her praises
          and Rome's.

Bizet, Georges. *Carmen* (1875)
Librettists: Henri Meilhac and Ludovic Halévy, after Prosper
  Mérimée
Publishers: Broude Bros., Dover, International, Kalmus, G.
  Schirmer

61   1. Act I, No. 3, "Avec la garde montante"
      2. 2-part boy's voices
      3. 2.5 minutes
      4. Easy
      5. As a relief detachment of troops enters the city, a
         gang of street urchins mimics their movements
         with its own "military" tune.

62   1. Act I, No. 4, "La cloche a sonné" (Chorus of
         Cigarette Girls)
      2. SATB
      3. 5 minutes
      4. Moderately Difficult
      5. As the factory workers enter on their noon break,
         the men sing about how they wait each day to
         make love to the women. The women sing of the
         joys of smoking, comparing the fleeting smoke
         rings with the fleeting attentions of the men.

63   1. Act I, No. 8, "Que se passe-t-il donc là-bas"
      2. SA; Zuniga (B)
      3. 5 minutes
      4. Moderately Difficult
      5. The women take sides for and against Carmen when
         Zuniga asks who started a fight.

64   1. Act IV, Nos. 25-26, "A deux cuartos" and "Les voici"
      2. STB divisi, children; several incidental soli
      3. 15 minutes
      4. Moderately Difficult
      5. An excited throng is waiting in the town square for
         the bullfight procession to enter the arena. The

excitement builds in the second chorus (No. 26) as the parade approaches.

N.B. Each chorus may be performed separately.

Bizet, Georges. *La Jolie Fille de Perth* (1867)
Librettists: J.H. Vernoy de Saint-Georges and J. Adenis, after Sir Walter Scott
Publisher: Editions Choudens
65   1. Act I, No. 2, "Que notre enclume résonne et fume"
        2. TBB
        3. 2.5 minutes
        4. Medium
        5. A brief "anvil" chorus, which takes place in the armourer's workshop.

66   1. Act II, No. 9, "Carnaval!"
        2. SATB
        3. 4 minutes
        4. Medium
        5. The well-known carnival chorus: boisterous, full-bodied writing.
        N.B. This chorus is reprised later in the same act.

Bizet, Georges. *Les pêcheurs de perles* (1863)
Librettists: Michel Carré and Eugène Cormon
Publishers: Broude Bros., Editions Choudens, Kalmus, G. Schirmer
67   1. Act I, Scene 1, "Sur la grève en-fu"
        2. SATB
        3. 13 minutes
        4. Moderately Difficult
        5. A feast is underway as the assembled fishermen celebrate chasing away the demons of the storm, enabling them to resume their livelihood. The scene includes a brief orchestral dance.

68 1. Act I, Scene 3, "Sois la bienvenue"
2. STB
3. 2.5 minutes
4. Medium
5. The villagers surround and welcome Leila, begging her to watch over and protect them.

69 1. Act II, Finale, "Quelle voix nous appelle"
2. SATB divisi
3. 5 minutes
4. Moderately Difficult
5. A self-contained choral excerpt near the beginning of the Finale. The villagers, disturbed by the approaching storm, call on Brahma to protect them.

70 1. Act III, Scene 2, "Dès que le soleil"
2. SATB; Nadir (T)
3. 13 minutes
4. Difficult
5. Nadir lies on a funeral pyre as savage dances and chants are taking place around him. The chorus waits eagerly for the spilling of blood, with repeated shouts to Brahma. Nadir, in a short middle section, exclaims that he would gladly die to save Leila; the chorus interrupts him, calling for the fire to be lit.

Blitzstein, Marc. *Regina* (1949)
Librettist: composer, after Lillian Hellman
Publisher: Chappell and Co.
71 1. Act II, Scene 2, "Sing Hubbard"
2. SATB
3. 5 minutes
4. Moderately Difficult
5. A delightful party song-cum drinking song-cum paean to the glorious Hubbard clan, this sparkling

chorus contains speaking parts, patter, and
Fledermaus-style gusto.

Boïldieu, François Adrien. *La Dame Blanche* (1825)
Librettist: Eugène Scribe, after Sir Walter Scott
Publishers: Broude Bros., Editions Choudens
72   1. Act I, No. 1, "Sonnez, sonnez"
        2. SATB divisi
        3. 2.5 minutes
        4. Medium
        5. A festive gathering is underway, celebrating the
           christening of Dickson's child.

73   1. Act III, No. 12, "Vive à jamais notre nouveau
           seigneur!"
        2. SATB divisi; Georges (T)
        3. 3.5 minutes
        4. Difficult
        5. A crowd has gathered to welcome Georges, the new
           owner of the grand house where this scene takes
           place. They sing to him a version of an old
           Scottish tune.
        N.B. This is the opening portion of a longer scene.
        The excerpt may be considerably lengthened by adding
        the aria for Georges (with chorus) that follows; the
        aria, however, is quite difficult, ending on a sustained
        high C.

Boito, Arrigo. *Mefistofele* (1868)
Librettist: composer, after Johann W. von Goethe
Publishers: Broude Bros., Kalmus, Ricordi
74   1. Prologue, "Ave, Signor"
        2. SATB dbl. choir
        3. 3.5 minutes
        4. Moderately Difficult
        5. Invisible choirs, following a flourish of trumpet
           fanfares, sing a hymn to the Lord of Creation.

75   1. Prologue, "Salve Regina"
       2. unison boy's voices, SATB
       3. 8 minutes
       4. Difficult
       5. The scene begins with a chorus of spirits and another of earthly penitents. It builds into an ensemble of magnificent proportions as the cherubim sing in "chattering" rhythms, accompanying the heavenly choirs in their continuing hymn to the Lord of Creation.

76   1. Act I, Scene 1, "Juhé, juhé"
       2. SATB divisi
       3. 4.5 minutes
       4. Moderately Difficult
       5. A group of peasants carouses and begins to dance the *obertas*, a Polish dance with a mazurka-like rhythm.

Boito, Arrigo. *Nerone* (1924)
Librettist: composer
Publishers: Broude Bros., Ricordi
77   1. Act IV, Scene 1, "Vittoria! Gloria!"
       2. TTBB
       3. 2.5 minutes
       4. Medium
       5. A mob has gathered in the area of the Roman games to cheer the victors and castigate the losers.

Borodin, Aleksander. *Prince Igor* (*Keyaze Igor*) (1890)
Librettist: composer, after Vladimir V. Stassov
Publishers: Belaieff (cw), Boosey and Hawkes, Broude Bros., G. Schirmer
78   1. Act I, Scene 1, "We know what happens to Poutivl"
       2. TTBB; Eroshka (T), Skoula (B)
       3. 4.5 minutes

4. Moderately Difficult
5. The peasants take account of the ills Igor has lately faced, with a keen awareness of the dangers their village of Poutivl is experiencing.

79   1. Act II, Nos. 7, 10, 17, "Polovetsian Dances"
      2. SATB
      3. 25 minutes
      4. Medium
      5. Scene No. 17 is usually excerpted as the well-known "Polovetsian Dances," but the two earlier numbers may be used as well.

80   1. Act III, Scene 1, "Polovetsian March"
      2. TTBB
      3. 3 minutes
      4. Moderately Difficult
      5. A rough, harsh chorus, much of it for unison male voices, but splitting into four parts at the end. The chorus is used in the opera to accompany the entrance of the Khan Gzak and his warriors.

81   1. Act III, No. 20b, "So haste we to seek your counsel"
      2. TTBB
      3. 2 minutes
      4. Medium
      5. A brief chorus of homage to Khan Kontchak.

82   1. Act IV, Finale, "A calm sky ends our pains"
      2. SATB; Eroshka (T), Skoula (B)
      3. 6 minutes
      4. Moderately Difficult
      5. The city has been saved and Igor has returned home, celebrated in this chorus of thanksgiving.

Boughton, Rutland. *The Immortal Hour* (1914)
Librettist: Fiona Macleod
Publisher: Stainer and Bell
83   1. Act I, Finale, "How beautiful they are"
        2. SATB divisi
        3. 3 minutes
        4. Medium
        5. A folk-like hymn, sung to "the lordly ones who
           dwell in the hills." The sopranos carry the melody
           and text, accompanied by the lower voices singing
           "la."

84   1. Act II, Scene 1, "By the voice in the corries"
        2. SSAA/TTBB dbl. choir
        3. 15 minutes
        4. Moderately Difficult
        5. The Druids enter the hall of the King's home,
           celebrating the year that has passed since he met
           Etain (S). A rather mystical text recalls the
           meeting and hopes for peace and prosperity. Large
           portions of this scene are unaccompanied.

Britten, Benjamin. *Billy Budd* (1951)
Librettist: E.M. Forster and Eric Crozier, after Herman
    Melville
Publishers: Broude Bros., Boosey and Hawkes
85   1. Act II, Scene 1, "This is our moment"
        2. TTBB divisi
        3. 6.5 minutes
        4. Difficult
        5. A wonderfully evocative chorus in which the British
           see naval action against the French. The men call
           upon all of their reserves of strength to fight, but
           the action ends indecisively for them.
        N.B. The excerpted scene runs from rehearsal nos. 15
        to 22; with the addition of a number of solo voices,
        this could be greatly extended.

Britten, Benjamin. *Death in Venice* (1973)
Librettist: Myfanwy Piper, after Thomas Mann
Publishers: Boosey and Hawkes, Faber, G. Schirmer
86   1. Act I, Scene 3, "Bride of the Sea, Serenissima"
        2. SATB divisi; several short solos
        3. 3 minutes
        4. Difficult
        5. During a journey by boat to the Lido in Venice, this
           quasi-aleatoric chorus is sung in the distance. In
           between sweet chants of "serenissima" are heard
           phrases of youthful love and courting.

87   1. Act I, Scene 4, "The Lido is so charming"
        2. SATB divisi; Aschenbach (T), several short solos
        3. 4 minutes
        4. Difficult
        5. In a delightful conglomeration of several languages
           and moods, a large group of hotel guests
           assembles for dinner. Several diverse snippets of
           conversation are overheard along the way.

88   1. Act I, Scene 7, "Beneath a dazzling sky"
        2. SATB divisi; The Voice of Apollo (Countertenor)
        3. 12 minutes
        4. Difficult
        5. A set of Olympic games, in which the youth Tadzio
           participates and wins, is the source for a set of
           commentary choruses reflecting on athletic beauty
           and ability, among other things. The scene takes
           place in Aschenbach's mind.

Britten, Benjamin. *Gloriana* (1953)
Librettist: William Plomer
Publishers: Boosey and Hawkes, Broude Bros.
89   1. Act II, Scene 1, "Choral Dances"
        2. SATB (various combinations); unaccompanied
        3. 2-13 minutes

4. Difficult
5. A series of six choral dances, sung by various combinations of voices. Each dance is an allegory referring to Time, Concord, Time and Concord, Flowers, Rustics, and a final dance of homage. These dances may be performed separately or together, with or without the connecting recitatives.

Britten, Benjamin. *A Midsummer Night's Dream* (1960)
Librettist: composer and Peter Pears, after William Shakespeare
Publishers: Boosey and Hawkes, Broude Bros.

90　1. Act I, "Over hill, over dale"
2. Sopranos or children's voices, divisi
3. 6 minutes
4. Medium
5. The Fairies frolic in the forest, celebrating their powers to wreak mischief among mortals.
N.B. One spoken line for Puck may be omitted without harm.

91　1. Act I, Finale, "You spotted snakes with double tongue"
2. Sopranos or children's voices, divisi
3. 3 minutes
4. Medium
5. Tytania calls upon the Fairies to sing her to sleep, which they do.

Britten, Benjamin. *Paul Bunyan* (1941; rev. 1974)
Librettist: W.H. Auden
Publishers: Boosey and Hawkes, Broude Bros., Faber

92　1. Prologue, "Since the birth of the earth"
2. SATB; SSTT and MMS soli
3. 12.5 minutes

4. Moderately Difficult
5. A chorus of Old Trees (SATB) joins the Young Trees (SSTT) and the Wild Geese (MMS) in a paean to the forces of nature, which Paul Bunyan will master. The symbolism refers to the taming of the young United States.

93   1. Act I, No. 4, "My birthplace was in Sweden"
      2. TTBB; several short soli
      3. 2.5 minutes
      4. Medium
      5. Lumberjacks brag of their manliness, sense of adventure, and importance.

94   1. Act I, Scene 2, "Food Chorus"
      2. TTBB; Innkeeper (T)
      3. 8 minutes
      4. Medium
      5. In this fast patter chorus, the lumberjacks complain about the quality of food in their camp.

Britten, Benjamin. *Peter Grimes* (1945)
Librettist: Montagu Slater, after George Crabbe
Publishers: Boosey and Hawkes, Broude Bros.
95   1. Act I, Scene 1, "Oh, hang at open doors the net"
      2. SATB
      3. 4 minutes
      4. Medium
      5. A series of three short choruses that can be sung together by ignoring the short intervening recitatives. In each chorus, the villagers sing quietly while they go about their work, preparing for another day of fishing.

96   1. Act I, Finale, "Old Joe has gone fishing"
      2. SATB
      3. 3.5 minutes

4. Medium
5. A rather boisterous round in 7/4, led by Ned Keene, intended in the opera to break the tension of the scene. Three different tunes are used in various patterns.

N.B. Actually written for soli and chorus, there is a separate octavo publication available from Boosey and Hawkes, arranged for chorus alone.

Britten, Benjamin. *The Rape of Lucretia* (1946)
Librettist: Ronald Duncan, after André Obey
Publishers: Boosey and Hawkes, Broude Bros., G. Schirmer

97   1. Act I, Interlude, "Tarquinias does not wait"
2. Unison male voices
3. 6 minutes
4. Moderately Difficult
5. A graphic chorus, depicting Tarquinias' flight to Lucretia's house in Rome. Wonderfully evocative, the chorus ends with a fierce cry of "Lucretia!"

98   1. Act I, Scene 2, "Time treads upon the hands of women"
2. Unison female voices; Lucia (S) Bianca (M)
3. 3.5 minutes
4. Moderately Difficult
5. The two soloists sing on "ah" while folding linen; the chorus comments on the importance of the routine, basic work done by all women.

99   1. Act II, Scene 1, "She sleeps as a rose upon the night"
2. Unison female voices
3. 2 minutes
4. Easy
5. A brief lullaby to Lucretia.

100   1. Act II, Interlude, "Here is this scene"
            2. SATB unison
            3. 3 minutes
            4. Medium
            5. A Christian moral, sung after the rape scene.

Busoni, Ferruccio. *Turandot* (1917)
Librettist: composer, after Gozzi
Publishers: Breitkopf & Härtel, Broude Bros., G. Schirmer
101   1. Act I, Scene 2, "Einzug des Kaisers"
            2. TTBB
            3. 2.5 minutes
            4. Easy
            5. Stately music announces the entrance of the
               Emperor, preceded by his wise doctors and various
               servants.

C

Catalani, Alfredo. *La Wally* (1892)
Librettist: Luigi Illica
Publishers: Broude Bros., Kalmus, Ricordi, G. Schirmer
102   1. Act II, Scene 1, "Entro la folla"
            2. SATB; several incidental soli
            3. 4.5 minutes
            4. Medium
            5. A festive party is underway at the Eagle Tavern,
               while the patrons await the arrival of Wally.

Chabrier, Alexis Emmanuel. *L'Étoile* (1877)
Librettists: E. Leterrier and A. Vanloo
Publishers: Enoch and Sons, Litolff's Verlag

103   1. Act I, Finale (No. 6a), "Le pal! le pal!"
        2. STB
        3. 2.5 minutes
        4. Medium
        5. The King has sent for instruments of torture to kill Lazuli, a Pedlar, who has inadvertently boxed the King's ears. The crowd delights in anticipation.

104   1. Act II, No. 12, "Nous alons donc voir"
        2. SATB
        3. 2.5 minutes
        4. Medium
        5. As Laoula tells her sad love story, the chorus empathizes with her.

105   1. Act II, Finale, "C'est malheur"
        2. SATB divisi
        3. 4.5 minutes
        4. Moderately Difficult
        5. In a continuation of the previous excerpt, the crowd further empathizes with Laoula. The chorus is rather tongue-in-cheek and fairly humorous.

Chabrier, Emmanuel. *Le Roi malgré lui* (1887)
Librettist: Emile de Najae and Paul Burani, after Ancelot
Publisher: Enoch and Co., LC

106   1. Act I, No. 1, "Soldiers' Chorus"
        2. SATB divisi and SATB semi-chorus
        3. 5 minutes
        4. Difficult
        5. A rousing soldier's chorus; the semi-chorus is soloistic in nature.
        N.B. A similar chorus occurs in the Finale of Act I.

107   1. Act II, No. 9, "Choral Dance"
        2. SATB divisi; Laski (Bar)

3. 8 minutes
4. Difficult
5. A choral dance, employing the familiar "fête
   polonaise."
N.B. The writing uses the extremes of all voice ranges.

Charpentier, Gustave. *Louise* (1900)
Librettist: composer
Publishers: Heugel, G. Schirmer
108 1. Act III, Scene 2, "Régalez-vous, mes dam's"
2. SATB mulitiple choirs, and boy's choir; Julien (T)
3. 13 minutes
4. Difficult
5. Julien's Bohemian companions steal into a garden
   and quietly begin decorating the front of a cottage
   with banners and streamers. Other merrymakers
   join them and soon a loud, raucous group has
   assembled for a carnival in honor of Louise and
   Julien.

Cherubini, Luigi. *Médée* (1797)
Librettist: François Benoit Hoffman, after Euripides
Publishers: Broude Bros., Ricordi, G. Schirmer
109 1. Act I, No. 4, "Wedding Chorus"
2. STTB; Glauce (S), Jason (T), Creon (B)
3. 5 minutes
4. Moderately Difficult
5. In a beautiful, tranquil piece, the solo trio calls the
   gods' blessings upon a forthcoming marriage,
   echoed by the chorus.
N.B. Much of the trio's music is doubled in the choral
parts.

110 1. Act II, Finale, "Ah! triste canto!"
2. SATB; Medea (S)
3. 11 minutes

4. Difficult
5. As the soldiers and citizens emerge from the temple after the wedding, Medea rages against the turn of events and, seizing a burning torch, runs with it offstage. A rather dramatic, skillfully handled scene.

Cornelius, Peter. *Der Barbier von Baghdad* (1858)
Librettist: composer
Publishers: Breitkopf & Härtel, Broude Bros., G. Schirmer
111   1. Act I, Scene 1, "Sanfter Schlummer"
2. TTBB; Nureddin (T)
3. 7.5 minutes
4. Moderately Difficult
5. Nureddin lies on a couch surrounded by his servants. He is dying of unrequited love and they worry over him with the greatest of anxiety.

112   1. Act I, Scene 6, "Hinaus!"
2. TTBB
3. 2.5 minutes
4. Moderately Difficult
5. Nurredin has ordered Abul out of his house and calls his servants to do his bidding. They oblige in this rousing, bustling chorus.
N.B. The scene may be slightly extended with Abul's reply (following), which the chorus punctuates.

113   1. Act I, Finale, "So lasset uns eilen"
2. TTBB
3. 2 minutes
4. Moderately Difficult
5. Nureddin's servants assure Abul (facetiously) that they only want to help him, when in fact they want to hinder his actions.

D

Dallapiccola, Luigi. *Il Prigioniero* (1949)
Librettist: composer
Publishers: Boosey and Hawkes, G. Schirmer, Edizioni Suvini
  Zerboni
114   1. First Choral Intermezzo, "Fiat, misericordia tua"
   2. SATB
   3. 2 minutes
   4. Moderately Difficult
   5. An offstage chorus interrupts a mother's ballad with
       a hymn, sung as she is waiting to visit her son in
       prison: "Let your mercy, O Lord, come upon us."

115   1. Second Choral Intermezzo, "Domine, labia mea
       aperies"
   2. SATB; Prisoner (Bar)
   3. 3.5 minutes
   4. Difficult
   5. As the Prisoner makes his escape, the chorus is
       heard singing a lush, grandiose hymn of praise,
       ending in a short "alleluia" by the prisoner, who
       marvels at the starlight, symbol of his freedom.

Delibes, Léo. *Lakmé* (1883)
Librettists: Edmond Gondinet and Philippe Gille
Publishers: Broude Bros., Heugel, International, G. Schirmer
116   1. Act II, No. 7, "Allons, avant que midi sonne"
   2. SATB divisi
   3. 6 minutes
   4. Moderately Difficult
   5. A festive chorus that takes place at an Indian
       bazaar.

Delius, Frederick. *A Village Romeo and Juliet* (1907)
Librettist: composer, after Gottfried Keller
Publishers: Boosey and Hawkes, Broude Bros., G. Schirmer
117　1. Scene 4, "Lord, before thy mighty will"
　　　2. SATB, organ
　　　3. 1.5 minutes
　　　4. Easy
　　　5. A short wedding hymn, calling God's blessing upon
　　　　the union.

Donizetti, Gaetano. *Anna Bolena* (1830)
Librettist: Felice Romani
Publishers: Broude Bros., Kalmus, Ricordi, G. Schirmer
118　1. Act II, Scene 1, "Oh! dove mai ne andarono"
　　　2. SA
　　　3. 3.5 minutes
　　　4. Medium
　　　5. Anna's ladies-in-waiting try to comfort her as she
　　　　awaits her fate in custody, assuring her that virtue
　　　　will save her in the end.

119　1. Act II, Scene 11, "Chi può verderla"
　　　2. SA
　　　3. 3 minutes
　　　4. Easy
　　　5. Anna's ladies-in-waiting express their grief and pity
　　　　as she waits for death.

Donizetti, Gaetano. *Don Pasquale* (1843)
Librettist: Giovanni Ruffini
Publishers: Broude Bros., Kalmus, Ricordi, G. Schirmer
120　1. Act III, Scene 3, "Che interminabile andirivieni"
　　　2. SATB divisi
　　　3. 5 minutes
　　　4. Moderately Difficult

5. The servants complain about being overworked in this delightful chorus, and at the same time gossip about what is going on "upstairs." They end by cautioning each other to be careful and alert so that they may continue to enjoy the advantages of working in a grand house.

Donizetti, Gaetano. *L'Elisir d'Amore* (1832)
Librettist: Felice Romani
Publishers: Broude Bros., Kalmus, Ricordi, G. Schirmer
121   1. Act I, Scene 1, "Bel conforto al mietitore"
      2. SATB divisi; Giannetta (S)
      3. 3 minutes
      4. Moderately Difficult
      5. A group of peasants sings of the pleasures of spending a restful hour in the cool shade.

122   1. Act I, Scene 4, "Che vuol dire cotesta"
      2. SATB
      3. 3 minutes
      4. Medium
      5. As a trumpet sounds in the distance, the peasants excitedly gather, exclaiming about a magnificent carriage approaching.

Donizetti, Gaetano. *La Favorita* (1840)
Librettists: Alphonse Royer and Gustav Vaez, after Baculard d'Arnaud
Publishers: Boosey and Hawkes, Broude Bros., Garland, Ricordi, G. Schirmer
123   1. Act III, No. 23, "Di già nella cappella"
      2. SATTB
      3. 2.5 minutes
      4. Medium
      5. Leonora is about to be married to Ferdinand, who doesn't know she has been the King's mistress. In

this chorus, the lords and ladies begin *sotto voce* to whisper jealously about the scandal, until their murmuring reaches a raucous *fortissimo*.

N.B. The opera was originally written in French; this chorus is reprised in No. 24b.

124   1. Act III, No. 25, "Oh! vitalde!"
2. TB; Don Gasparo (T)
3. 4 minutes
4. Medium
5. Futher approbrations regarding the scandal (see annotation above).

N.B. Much of Gasparo's music is doubled in the tenor choral part.

Donizetti, Gaetano. *La Figlia del Reggimento* (1840)
Librettists: Bayard and Jules H. Vernoy
Publishers: Broude Bros., Kalmus, Ricordi, G. Schirmer, Universal Edition

125   1. Act I, No. 6, "Sprona il tamburo"
2. TTB
3. 2.5 minutes
4. Medium
5. A roll of drums calls the soldiers to quarters and they sing this martial chorus as they leave camp.

126   1. Act I, No. 9, "Rataplan"
2. TTB; Corporal (Bar)
3. 3 minutes
4. Medium
5. A regiment of soldiers enters stage singing a stirring military chorus that champions the glory of combat and victory.

Donizetti, Gaetano. *Linda di Chamounix* (1842)
Librettist: Gaetano Rossi
Publishers: Broude Bros., Kalmus, G. Schirmer
127   1. Act III, Scene 1, "Viva!"
      2. SATB; several short solos
      3. 4 minutes
      4. Moderately Difficult
      5. In the square, the villagers of Chamounix have gathered to welcome home the returning Savoyards. Shouts of joy are intermingled with family reunions, and the scene ends with a lively *brindisi* or toast.

Donizetti, Gaetano. *Lucia di Lammermoor* (1835)
Librettist: Salvatore Cammarano, after Sir Walter Scott
Publishers: Broude Bros., Kalmus, Ricordi, G. Schirmer
128   1. Act II, No. 8, "Per te d'immenso giubilo"
      2. STB divisi; Sir Arthur Bucklaw (T)
      3. 7.5 minutes
      4. Moderately Difficult
      5. The chorus sings a hymn of praise and congratulations to Sir Arthur, who is about to marry the unwilling Lucia.

129   1. Act III, No. 12, "D'immenso giubilo"
      2. STB divisi; one short B solo
      3. 4 minutes
      5. Medium
      6. A continuation of the previous chorus: here, the gathered celebrate the wedding of Lucia to Arthur, after the earlier ceremony ended abruptly in accusations and recriminations.

Donizetti, Gaetano. *Lucrezia Borgia* (1833)
Librettist: Felice Romani, after Victor Hugo
Publishers: Broude Bros., Kalmus, Novello, Ricordi, G.
  Schirmer
130   1. Act II, No. 18, "Stolti! ei corre alla Negroni"
      2. SATB; Rustighello (T)
      3. 2.5 minutes
      4. Easy
      5. The final chorus of the opera, which functions
         moralistically: "Madmen! they hasten to destruc-
         tion. . .leave them, they rush to their own ruin."

Donizetti, Gaetano. *Maria Stuarda* (1834)
Librettist: Giuseppe Bardari
Publishers: Kalmus, G. Schirmer
131   1. Act I, No. 1, "Qui s'attenda"
      2. SATB
      3. 2.5 minutes
      4. Medium
      5. A festival is underway at the Palace of Westminster,
         where the guests anticipate the arrival of Queen
         Elizabeth, who they think will unite the thrones of
         England and France through marriage (which she
         promptly avows not to do in the succeeding
         cavatina).

132   1. Act III, No. 16, "Vedeste? Vedemo"
      2. SATB divisi
      3. 4.5 minutes
      4. Moderately Difficult
      5. Mary's supporters, on hearing of her impending
         death at the behest of Elizabeth, protest this crime
         against a woman they perceive as an innocent
         victim. They assert that with this deed England
         will live in infamy forever.

Donizetti, Gaetano. *Roberto Deveroux* (1837)
Librettist: Salvatore Cammarano, after Ancelot
Publishers: Alexander Broude, Egret House (cw), Garland,
   Ricordi
133   1. Act II, Scene 1, "L'ore trascorrono"
         2. SATB
         3. 5 minutes
         4. Medium
         5. In the hall of the Westminster palace, the lords and
            ladies of Elizabeth's court wait with some
            apprehension to hear of Roberto's fate, which they
            consider lost, saying that with her silence, the
            Queen condemns him to death.

Dukas, Paul. *Ariane et Barbe-bleue* (1907)
Librettist: composer, after Maurice Mäterlinck
Publisher: Durand
134   1. Act I, Scene 1, "A mort! A mort!"
         2. SATB/TTBB dbl. chorus
         3. 5.5 minutes
         4. Difficult
         5. An angry, offstage crowd is agitating outside
            Bluebeard's castle. They think he has murdered
            his wives one after the other and are fearful that
            Ariane may be next.
N.B. There is no clear ending for this chorus, although
two or three spots seem possible; the conductor
should not have trouble finding a suitable place.

Dvořák, Antonín. *The Water Nymph* (*Rusalka*) (1901)
Librettist: S. Jaroslava Kvapil
Publishers: Broude Bros., Export-Artia (Prague), Hudební
   Matice (cw)
135   1. Act II, No. 9, "White flowers are blooming"
         2. SATB
         3. 3.5 minutes

4. Medium
5. A delightful, folksong-inspired chorus, sung while
   the Old Spirit of the Lake is mourning for his
   daughter. The chorus functions as a wedding song
   for the Prince, who will marry someone other than
   the Old Spirit's daughter.
   N.B. The chorus is reprised shortly following, in
   quodlibet with the Old Spirit's lament.

136 1. Act III, No. 7, "Golden is my hair"
2. SSAA
3. 3 minutes
4. Medium
5. A chorus of water nymphs pities the daughter of the
   Spirit of the Lake; she has assumed human form
   in order to marry the Prince, who no longer
   desires her.

E

Einem, Gottfried von. *Dantons Tod* (1947)
Librettists: composer and Boris Blacher, after Büchner
Publishers: Broude Bros., G. Schirmer, Universal Edition
137 1. Act I, Scene 2, "Ja, ein Messer!"
2. SATB; Ein junge Mensch (T)
3. 4.5 minutes
4. Difficult
5. An angry crowd grabs a young aristocrat and is
   about to hang him. He offers them a clever turn of
   phrase and their anger changes to cheers of
   "bravo!" at his wit.

F

Falla, Manuel de. *La Vida Breve* (1913)
Librettist: C. Fernandez Shaw
Publishers: J.W. Chester, Max Eschig, B. Schott's Söhne, G.
  Schirmer
138   1. Act II, Scene 3, (no title or text)
       2. SATB
       3. 7 minutes
       4. Medium
       5. An exception to the guidelines presented in the
          Guide to Use at the front of this volume, this
          exciting but wordless chorus is too good to be left
          out. A fiesta is in full swing and the boisterous
          guests sing and shout with abandon.

Fauré, Gabriel. *Pénélope* (1900)
Librettist: René Fauchois
Publisher: Heugel
139   1. Act I, Scene 1, "Les fuseaux sont lourds"
       2. SA
       3. 2.5 minutes
       4. Easy
       5. This simple chorus is sung by Pénélope's serving
          women, who gleefully proclaim that they, unlike
          their mistress, would be unable to resist the
          charms of all Pénélope's suitors and would have
          succumbed to them long ago. Much of the chorus
          is in unison, often constructed in a question and
          answer style.

Flotow, Friedrich von. *Martha* (1847)
Librettist: Friedrich Wilhelm Riese
Publishers: Breitkopf & Härtel, Broude Bros., Kalmus, G.
  Schirmer, Josef Weinberger

140   1. Act I, No. 1, "Darf mit nächtig düstern Träumen"
2. SSA; Lady Harriet (S), Nancy (A)
3. 3.5 minutes
4. Medium
5. The women of young Lady Harriet's boudoir urge her to drive away her melancholy by taking part in the whirl of pleasures at court.

141   1. Act I, No. 4, "Mädchen, brav und treu"
2. SATB divisi/SSA dbl. chorus
3. 5.5 minutes
4. Medium
5. The scene takes place at the Richmond fair, where the farmers urge the servant girls to appear at their best when the men bid at auction for the girls' services. The servant girls sing about the traditional fees they will get at the auction.

G

Gershwin, George. *Porgy and Bess* (1935)
Librettist: DuBose Heyward
Publishers: Broude Bros., Chappell and Co.
142   1. Act I, Scene 2, "Where is brudder Robbins?"
2. SAATBB; several short solos
3. 3 minutes
4. Moderately Difficult
5. A chorus of mourners watches over Robbins's body as it lies in Serena's room.
N.B. This scene may be significantly extended with the addition of several solo sections for Porgy (B), Bess (S), and others.

143   1. Act I, Scene 2, Finale, "Oh, we're leavin' for the
              Promise' Lan'"
           2. SAATBB
           3. 5 minutes
           4. Moderately Difficult
           5. A rousing spiritual, accompanying Robbins's body to
              the undertakers, reaffirms a belief in the hereafter.
           N.B. This scene may be extended backwards for
           several minutes by adding Bess's preceding solo with
           its choral accompaniment.

144   1. Act II, Scene 1, "Oh, I can't sit down"
           2. SATB
           4. 3 minutes
           4. Medium
           5. A sunny, jaunty chorus sung on the way to a picnic
              in town.

145   1. Act II, Scene 2, "I ain't got no shame" and "It ain't
              necessarily so"
           2. SATB; Sporting Life (T)
           3. 7 minutes
           4. Medium
           5. A celebratory chorus, accompanied by African
              drum, leads into the famous song and chorus for
              Sporting Life.

Ginastera, Alberto. *Bomarzo* (1967)
Librettist: Manuel Mujica Lainez
Publishers: Boosey and Hawkes; Indiana University School of
   Music
146   1. Act I, Scene 6, "O Rex gloriae"
           2. SATB
           3. 3 minutes
           4. Medium

5. A short anthem to Pier Francesco Orsini, sung as he accepts the responsibilities of succeeding to a Dukedom.

147   1. Act II, Scene 10, "Todo ed aire espejea"
      2. SAT
      3. 2 minutes
      4. Difficult
      5. A lyrical wedding song to Julia and Pier Francesco.

148   1. Act II, Interlude 12, "Si quieres saber de mí"
      2. SATB unaccompanied
      3. 2 minutes
      4. Difficult
      5. A polyphonic choral *vilanella* about love.

Giordano, Umberto. *Andrea Chénier* (1896)
Librettist: Luigi Illica
Publishers: Broude Bros., International, G. Schirmer

149   1. Act I, "O pastorella"
      2. SSA(T)
      3. 3 minutes
      4. Medium
      5. In a play-within-a-play, a group of shepherdesses sings their folk-like pastoral, a "shepherds' farewell." The tenors, who enter near the end, are part of the audience watching the play; their part may be omitted without harm.

150   1. Act III, "Amici, ancor cantram"
      2. STB
      3. 1.5 minutes
      4. Easy
      5. A setting of a revolutionary song and dance, the Carmagnole. The basses sing first, answered by the sopranos then the tenors in unison, all on the same text but in different keys.

Glinka, Michael. *Ivan Susanin* (*A Life for the Tsar*) (1836)
Librettist: G.F. Rosen
Publishers: Durdilly, Kalmus, Moscow State Music Publishers
   (cw)

151   1. Act I, Scene 1, "Like the middle of the storm"
         2. SATB
         3. 8 minutes
         4. Moderately Difficult
         5. A lengthy patriotic chorus sung by the peasants as
            they welcome back to the village Sobinin, the
            fiance of Antonida, Susanin's daughter.

152   1. Act II, Scene 1, "Strong soldiers"
         2. SATB
         3. 6.5 minutes
         4. Medium
         5. A long and boisterous chorus, sung by Polish
            soldiers at a ball, where they look forward to
            victory in their coming campaign against the
            Russians.

153   1. Act II, Finale, "Fortune conspires against us"
         2. SATB/TB dbl. choir
         3. 12.5 minutes
         4. Moderately Difficult
         5. A mood of anger and rage turns into a celebration
            of imminent victory, as the Poles become
            convinced they will capture the newly crowned
            Tsar of Russia, assuring their success and salvaging
            their honor.

154   1. Epilogue, "To the Russians, honor and glory!"
         2. SATB triple choir
         3. 6 minutes
         4. Moderately Difficult
         5. A grand, magnificent chorus of celebration as the
            Tsar enters the Kremlin palace in triumph. His life

has been saved through the patriotism and courage
of Ivan Susanin.

155 1. Epilogue, Finale, "God, who leads our noble Tsar to
        honor"
     2. SATB dbl. choir
     3. 8.5 minutes
     4. Moderately Difficult
     5. A final chorus of homage and celebration, to both
        Russia and the Tsar.

Glinka, Michael. *Russlan and Lyudmila* (1842)
Librettists: V.F. Shirkov and K.A. Bakhturnin, after Alexander
  Pushkin
Publishers: Boosey and Hawkes, Kalmus, Moscow State Music
  Publishers (cw), Editioni Suvini Zerboni
156 1. Act I, No. 1, "To you prince, glory and greetings"
     2. SAB
     3. 5.5 minutes
     4. Medium
     5. A bard has prophesied good things for Lyudmila
        and Russlan, one of her suitors, including glory for
        their beloved Kiev, whose ruler is Svietosar,
        Lyudmila's father. The chorus sings in celebration.

157 1. Act IV, No. 21, "For in learning, there is struggle"
     2. SATB
     3. 7.5 minutes
     4. Moderately Difficult
     5. An agitated chorus where the people worry and
        wonder who will win the battle for Lyudmila:
        Russlan or Tchernomor, an evil dwarf.

158 1. Act V, Finale, "Glory to God in the Heavens!"
     2. SATB
     3. 4.5 minutes
     4. Medium

5. Russlan breaks a spell over the long-sleeping Lyudmila with the aid of a magic ring. The peasants rejoice and celebrate.

N.B. This chorus appears several times in various lengths in this scene. The annotated excerpt uses approximately the last 100 measures of the opera (not including repeats.)

Gluck, Christoph Willibald von. *Alceste* (1767)
Librettist: Ranieri di Calzabigi
Publishers: Bärenreiter, Breitkopf & Härtel, Broude Bros., Heugel, Kalmus, Ricordi

159
1. Act II, Scene 1, "Que les plus doux transports"
2. SATB; 4 soli (SATB)
3. 2 minutes
4. Medium
5. A short chorus of thanks to the gods, and of praise to Admetus, their sovereign.

N.B. A different version of this chorus, without soloists, occurs after an intervening ballet. The two choruses might be sung separately or together.

160
1. Act II, Scene 2, "O malheureux Admète!"
2. SATB dbl. choir
3. 2.5 minutes
4. Medium
5. The two choruses comment upon the cursed fate of Alceste's sons and call down the protection of the gods upon them.

N.B. The chorus is reprised shortly following this scene.

161
1. Act II, Scene 3, "Livrons nous à l'allégresse"
2. SATB; 4 soli (SATB), Alceste (S)
3. 2.5 minutes
4. Medium

5. The crowd continues to laud Admetus. Alceste, in her single line, complains that their continued cheers bring pain to her heart.

162   1. Act III, Finale, "Qu'ils vivent à jamais"
      2. SATB; 4 soli (SATB)
      3. 3 minutes
      4. Easy
      5. A final chorus of joy and thanksgiving, calling down blessing and happiness upon Alceste and Admetus.

Gluck, Christoph Willibald von. *Iphigénie en Aulide* (1774)
Librettist: Bailli du Rollet (Roullet)
Publishers: Bärenreiter, Broude Bros., Editions Choudens

163   1. Act I, Scene 5, "Que d'attraits, que de majesté"
      2. SATB
      3. 4 minutes
      4. Medium
      5. A crowd of people welcomes Clytemnestre and Iphigénie as they arrive on the island of Aulide.

164   1. Act II, Scene 3, "Ami sensible, ennemi redoutable"
      2. SATB
      3. 3 minutes
      4. Medium
      5. A martial chorus, in which the Greeks warn the Phyrigians to beware of their power and determination.

165   1. Act III, Scene 8, "Jusque aux voûtes éthérées"
      2. SATB
      3. 4 minutes
      4. Medium
      5. A chorus of celebration marking the "glorious triumph" of the Greeks as they set sail for home, having appeased the gods and reconciled all the principal characters one to another.

Gluck, Christoph Willibald von. *Iphigénie en Tauride* (1779)
Librettist: François Guillard
Publishers: Bärenreiter, Boosey and Hawkes, Broude Bros.,
    Editions Choudens, Eulenberg, Jerona, Kalmus
166   1. Act III, Scene 2, "Hymne"
       2. SA
       3. 2 minutes
       4. Easy
       5. A short, simple hymn to the goddess Diana, asking
          for peace.

167   1. Act IV, Finale, "Les Dieux, longtemps en couroux"
       2. SATB
       3. 3 minutes
       4. Easy
       5. A hymn of thanks to the gods, who have granted
          the people's wishes and have restored a peace
          "sweet and profound."

Gluck, Christoph Willibald von. *Orfeo ed Euridice* (1762)
Librettist: Ranieri da Calzabigi
Publishers: Bärenreiter, Broude Bros., Kalmus, Ricordi, G.
    Schirmer
168   1. Act I, No., 1, "Ah! se intorno a quest' urna funesta"
       2. SATB
       3. 2.5 minutes
       4. Medium
       5. Shepherds and nymphs place garlands on Euridice's
          tomb, calling upon her spirit to look down with
          pity on her husband, Orpheus.

169   1. Act II, Nos. 18, 21, "Chi mai dell' Erbo"
       2. SATB
       3. 5 minutes
       4. Medium
       5. Preceded by and later briefly interrupted by short
          instrumental "Dances of the Furies," these two

short choruses of Furies boldly ask who dares approach the gates of the underworld.

170 1. Act II, No. 23, "Misero giovane"
2. SATB
3. 1 minute
4. Easy
5. In a slow, somber chorus, the spirits ask Orpheus why he has come to this desolate place, the underworld.

171 1. Act II, No. 27, "Le porte stridano"
2. SATB
3. 4 minutes
4. Easy
5. The Furies succumb to Orpheus's pleading and command the portals of the underworld be opened.

172 1. Act II, Nos. 34, 37, "Vieni a' regni del riposo" and "Torno, o bella, al tuo consorte"
2. SATB
3. 4 minutes
4. Medium
5. In this pair of choruses, the Shades first reassure Orpheus that Euridice will be returned to him, and in the second chorus they lead her to Orpheus as the curtain falls.

Gounod, Charles. *Faust* (1859, rev. 1869)
Librettists: Jules Barbier and Michel Carré
Publishers: Broude Bros., Editions Choudens, Kalmus, Ricordi, G. Schirmer
N.B. The reader is advised that there are several variants of this opera, especially concerning the order of the acts and numbering of scenes. These annotations were written using the Schirmer score.

173   1. Act I, Scene 2, "Vin ou bière, bière ou vin"
        2. SATB divisi; Wagner (B)
        3. 9.5 minutes
        4. Moderately Difficult
        5. The well-known fair scene. Students sing and laugh,
           reveling in their carefree youth, much to the
           dismay of Faust who curses his advancing age.

174   1. Act I, Finale, "Ain-si que la brise légère"
        2. SATB
        3. 3 minutes
        4. Medium
        5. Another well-known chorus from the operatic
           repertory, often referred to as the "Faust Waltz."
           While it appears several times during the final
           scene, the most easily excerptable is its last
           appearance, also the longest setting.

175   1. Act III, Scene 3, "Gloire immortelle"
        2. TTBB
        3. 6 minutes
        4. Moderately Difficult
        5. A soldier's chorus sung by men returning from war.
           It is yet another familiar chorus from this opera,
           and one of the best examples in this genre. Set in
           12/8, the chorus literally struts with patriotism.

Gounod, Charles. *Mirelle* (1864)
Librettist: Michel Carré, after Frédéric Mistral
Library Location: LC
176   1. Act II, No. 3a, "La farandole"
        2. STB divisi
        3. 7 minutes
        4. Medium
        5. The *farandole* is a Provençal dance. Here, the
           chorus sings of its power to drive away care and
           worry.

N.B. The chorus is reprised at the end of the scene, No. 3c.

177 1. Act III, No. 12, "Marche et choeur"
     2. STB divisi
     3. 2.5 minutes
     4. Easy
     5. A short prayer said in the church of St. Mary, asking for protection and guidance.

Gounod, Charles. *Roméo et Juliette* (1867)
Librettists: Jules Barbier and Michel Carré, after William Shakespeare
Publishers: Broude Bros., Kalmus, G. Schirmer
178 1. Prologue, "Vérone vit jadis deux familles rivales"
     2. SATB
     3. 2.5 minutes
     4. Medium
     5. The chorus, including all the principals in the drama about to unfold, comments on the feud between the Capulets and the Montagues and the tragic love of Romeo and Juliet.

179 1. Act I, No. 1, "L'heure s'envole"
     2. SATB divisi
     3. 4.5 minutes
     4. Moderately Difficult
     5. The scene is the ballroom of the Capulets' house, where the assembled guests sing a lilting waltz reflecting the gaiety of the evening.

H

Halévy, Jacques François. *La Juive* (1835)
Librettist: Eugène Scribe
Publishers: Breitkopf & Härtel, Broude Bros., Editions
  Choudens, Garland, G. Schirmer
180   1. Act I, No. 1., "Hosanna, plaisir, ivresse"
           2. SATB
           3. 3 minutes
           4. Moderately Difficult
           5. From the church, a magnificent prayer pours out as
              Mass ends. The congregation, with much force and
              dignity, asks that their prayers ascend to the
              heavens. The chorus is rated moderately difficult
              mostly for its very high soprano tessitura.

181   1. Act I, No. 4, "Hàtons-nous, car l'heure s'avance" and
              "Ah! quel heureux destin"
           2. SATB and TTBB
           3. 14 minutes
           4. Medium
           5. These two choruses are directly juxtaposed, but they
              may be done either together or separately. They
              occur during a scene celebrating a holiday
              proclaimed by the Emperor.

182   1. Act III, No. 13, "Ô jour mémorable"
           2. SATTB
           3. 2.5 minutes
           4. Medium
           5. A festival is underway in some "magnificent
              gardens." The guests sing of the sumptuous
              banquet in honor of their prince, Leopold, and
              praise the "glory of the Emperor."

183   1. Act V, No. 20, "Quel plaisir! quelle joie!"
           2. SATTB

3. 9 minutes
4. Moderately Difficult
5. A crowd has gathered to witness the execution of two Jews who refuse to renouce their faith and accept Christianity. The chorus begins rather haltingly, but quickly accelerates in pace as the crowd becomes more agitated and accusatory. A haunting and disturbing chorus.

Handel, George Frideric.
N.B. Nearly all of these choruses conclude the operas from which they are taken. Originally, of course, they would have been sung by the combined principals of the cast. They are included here primarily for their accessibility to younger choruses.

Handel, George Frideric. *Alcina* (1735)
Librettist: A. Marchi
Publisher: Gregg Press (cw)
184   1. Act I, Scene 2, "Questo e'il ciel"
2. SATB
3. 4 minutes
4. Medium
5. Actually two versions of the same chorus. The first is marked *larghetto* and the second *presto*. They should not be performed together. The action takes place at the court of Alcina, a sorceress.

Handel, George Frideric. *Ariodante* (1735)
Librettist: Antonio Salvi, after Ariosto
Publisher: Gregg Press (cw)
185   1. Act III, Finale, "Ogn'uno acclami"
2. SATB
3. 4 minutes
4. Medium

5. A somewhat more difficult chorus than the others
   annotated here. This gala scene celebrates the
   reunion of Ariodante and Ginerva after the latter
   has be reprieved from death by the King.

Handel, George Frideric. *Giulio Cesare* (1724)
Librettist: Nicola Haym
Publishers: Broude Bros., Dover, Gregg Press (cw),
   International, Kalmus
186   1. Act III, Finale, "Ritorni o mai nel nostro core"
         2. SATB; Cleopatra (S), Cesare (T)
         3. 3 minutes
         4. Medium
         5. A happy chorus of rejoicing for Cleopatra's and
            Ceasar's triumph, sung at the harbor in
            Alexandria. A solo passage by the two principals
            briefly interrupts the choral portions of this scene.

Handel, George Frideric. *Rodelinda* (1725)
Librettist: Nicola Haym, after Antonio Salvi
Publisher: Gregg Press (cw)
187   1. Act III, Finale, "Dopo al notte oscura"
         2. SATB
         3. 3 minutes
         4. Easy
         5. The people rejoice as Rodelinda, the Queen of
            Lombardy, is restored to her throne.

Handel, George Frideric. *Serse* (*Xerxes*) (1738)
Librettists: Nicolo Minato and Silvio Stampiglia
Publishers: Bärenreiter, Gregg Press (cw), Kalmus
188   1. Act III, Finale, "Ritorno a noi la calma"
         2. SATB
         3. 2 minutes
         4. Easy

5. A typical celebratory chorus, sung after everyone
has been reunited, forgiven, and blessed. In a jolly
6/8.

Handel, George Frideric. *Tamerlano* (1724)
Librettist: Nicola Haym
Publisher: Gregg Press (cw)
189   1. Act III, Finale, "D'atra notte già mirasi a scorno"
      2. SATB
      3. 2.5 minutes
      4. Easy
      5. A *da capo* chorus, celebrating love.

Henze, Hans Werner. *Die Bassariden* (1966)
Librettists: W.H. Auden and Chester Kallman
Publishers: Associated Music Publishers, B. Schott's Söhne
190   1. Act I, Scene 1, "Pentheus ist unser Herr"
      2. SATB
      3. 8 minutes
      4. Difficult
      5. A long chorus of tribute by the citizens of Thebus
to their new lord. The chorus is rhythmically and
melodically rather straightforward, although it
demands a high tessitura. There is much textual
and some musical repetition.

Henze, Hans Werner. *König Hirsch* (1956)
Librettist: Heinz von Cramer, after Carlo Gonzi
Publishers: Associated Music Publishers, B. Schott's Söhne
191   1. Act III, Finale, "Komm Zeit! Komm gute
       Königszeit!"
      2. SSATBB, children's voices
      3. 2 minutes
      4. Difficult

   5. A very short chorus of general rejoicing by the
      peasants of a village, who celebrate the restoration
      of their king, Leandro, who had been turned into a
      stag through evil magic.

Hindemith, Paul. *Cardillac* (1926; rev. 1952)
Librettist: Ferdinand Lion, after E.T.A. Hoffmann
Publishers: Broude Bros., G. Schirmer, B. Schott's Söhne
192   1. Act I, Scene 1, "Notschrei! Aufstand!"
          2. SATB
          3. 6.5 minutes
          4. Difficult
          5. As the curtain rises, a Paris mob has taken angrily
             to the streets, seeking a mass-murderer and
             looking anywhere for a convenient victim.

Hindemith, Paul. *Mathis der Mahler* (1938)
Librettist: composer
Publishers: Broude Bros., G. Schirmer, B. Schott's Söhne
193   1. Tableau II, Scene 1, "Dem Volk stopft man die
             falschen"
          2. SATB in four choirs; Capito (T), Pommersfelden
             (B)
          3. 12 minutes
          4. Difficult
          5. Groups of Catholics, Lutherans, humanist students,
             and townspeople argue in a town hall, while the
             two principals try to keep order among them. A
             fascinating chorus, with accusations running thick
             between the various factions.

194   1. Tableau VI, Scene 2, "Dein ärgster Feind sitzt in dir
             selbst"
          2. SATB
          3. 8.5 minutes
          4. Difficult

5. Matthew, who has momentarily stopped in the woods while in flight, reflects that his life is much akin to the picture he just painted. This chorus recalls the demons tempting St. Anthony in that painting, portrayed through fast, biting rhythms and a quick tempo.

Humperdinck, Engelbert. *Königskinder* (1910)
Librettist: Ernst Rosmer
Publisher: Max Brockhaus
195   1. Act II, "Die Ratsherrn Kommen!"
      2. SATB
      3. 2 minutes
      4. Medium
      5. The people in an inn jump from their chairs in excitement when they think the King is coming, in this lively but brief chorus.
N.B. A very approachable chorus, but with a much higher tessitura at the end than the beginning.

J

Janáček, Leoš. *Jenůfa* (1904)
Librettist: composer, after Gabriella Preissová
Publishers: Broude Bros., G. Schirmer, Universal Edition
196   1. Act III, Scene 6, "Oh, mother"
      2. SA
      3. 3 minutes
      4. Easy
      5. A folksong-like wedding chorus, sung by young girls to Jenůfa. Very accessible to young choirs.

L

Lalo, Edouard. *Le Roi d'Ys* (1888)
Librettist: Edouard Blau
Publisher: Heugel
197   1. Act I, "Noël"
       2. SATB divisi; Jahel (Bar)
       3. 9 minutes
       4. Moderately Difficult
       5. A joyful Christmas chorus celebrating the end of the
          war and the peace brought to the people by the
          betrothal of the King's daughter to their enemy
          leader.

Lortzing, Albert. *Der Wildschütz* (1842)
Librettist: composer, after A. von Kotzebue
Publishers: Broude Bros., Litolff's Verlag, G. Schirmer; OSU
198   1. Act I, No. 5, "Seht dort den muntern Jäger"
       2. TTBB; Baron (T), Count (Bar)
       3. 3.5 minutes
       4. Medium
       5. A jolly hunting chorus, complete with "tra-ras" at
          the end. The lines for the two principals are often,
          but not always, doubled in the choral parts.

199   1. Act III, No. 14, "Um die Laube zu schmücken"
       2. SAA
       3. 2.5 minutes
       4. Medium
       5. Near the end of the opera, a group of young
          women sings of the wonders of falling in love. The
          excerpt ends with a tonal shift (A major to F
          major), but the performer can easily change the
          final chord to A major for a satisfactory
          conclusion.

200   1. Act III, Finale, "Unser Herr lebe hoch"
        2. SATB
        3. 3 minutes
        4. Medium
        5. The peasants, huntsmen, villagers, etc., sing a
           rousing chorus of praise to the Count.

Lortzing, Albert. *Zar und Zimmerman* (1837)
Librettist: composer
Publishers: Breitkopf & Härtel, Broude Bros., Kalmus, G.
  Schirmer
201   1. Act II, No. 1, "Hoch lebe die Freude!"
        2. SATB
        3. 4.5 minutes
        4. Medium
        5. A lively festival is underway, attended by the court
           and guests of Tsar Peter I. Somewhat like a
           drinking chorus, although there are also references
           to joy, love, and good food.

202   1. Act III, final, "Schmücket mit Kränzen und Blumen"
        2. SATB
        3. 3 minutes
        4. Medium
        5. The populace of the village sings a chorus of love
           and praise to the Tsar as he takes leave of them.

M

Martinu, Bohuslav. *The Greek Passion* (*Recke Pasije*) (1961)
Librettist: composer, after Nikos Kazantzakis
Publisher: Universal Edition
203   1. Act I, No. 2, "Grigoris/Hör unser flehn"

2. SATB dbl. choir
3. 1.5 minutes
4. Difficult
5. Two choruses (villagers and refugees) greet the
     priest Grigoris and ask God for mercy.

204   1. Act IV, Scene 1, "Kommt her und singt"
        2. SATB
        3. 1.5 minutes
        4. Difficult
        5. A lively wedding chorus.

Mascagni, Pietro. *Cavalleria Rusticana* (1890)
Librettists: G. Menasci and G. Targioni-Tozzetti
Publishers: Broude Bros., Kalmus, G. Schirmer
205   1. Scene 1, "Gli aranci olezzano sui verdi margini"
        2. SATB
        3. 7 minutes
        4. Medium
        5. The villagers sing of the splendors of nature and the
             new-born spring on Easter morning.

206   1. Scene 3, "Regina coeli"
        2. SATB dbl. choir
        3. 3.5 minutes
        4. Moderately Difficult
        5. A chorus from inside the chuch sings a motet that
             segues into an "external" (onstage) chorus singing
             a hymn to "Christ, whose glory breaks the gloom."
        N.B. With the addition of several solo voices, the
        scene may be significantly extended.

207   1. Scene 6, "Viva il vino spumeggiante"
        2. SATB divisi
        3. 2 minutes
        4. Medium
        5. An anthem to the glories of wine.

Mascagni, Pietro. *Iris* (1898)
Librettist: Luigi Illica
Publishers: Broude Bros., Ricordi, G. Schirmer
208   1. Act I, Scene 1, "Son io"
      2. SATB divisi
      3. 4.5 minutes
      4. Moderately Difficult
      5. As the sun rises (portrayed in the overture) a chorus sings one of the principal textual themes of the opera: "in warmth and light, there are light and love."

209   1. Act II, Finale, "Oh, maraviglia"
      2. SATB
      3. 3.5 minutes
      4. Moderately Difficult
      5. Iris has been abducted and taken (unaware) to a geisha house. As she steps onto a balcony, the crowd below cries out in amazement over her beauty, comparing her to a flower.

Massenet, Jules. *Don Quichotte* (1910)
Librettist: Henri Clan, after Miguel de Cervantes
Publishers: Broude Bros., Heugel
210   1. Act I, No. 5, "Allégresse! Vive Don Quichotte de la Manche!"
      2. SATB
      3. 3 minutes
      4. Medium
      5. A brief chorus of praise from the villagers to their hero. Very repetitive.

211   1. Act III, Scene 5, "Ah! voir un corps long"
      2. TTBB
      3. 2.5 minutes
      4. Medium

5. Bandits make fun of Quichotte, saying his lean, old body cannot instill much fear in his enemies.

Menotti, Gian Carlo. *The Saint of Bleeker Street* (1954)
Librettist: composer
Publisher: G. Schirmer
212   1. Act I, Scene 1, "Salve virgo florens"
        2. SATB
        3. 2 minutes
        4. Moderately Difficult
        5. As the ill Assunta is brought to center stage, the neighbors sing this prayer, calling on Mary's help to cure the ill woman.

213   1. Act III, Finale, "Kyrie eleison"
        2. SAATB
        3. 2 minutes
        4. Medium
        5. The text of the Kyrie and an Alleluia, sung as Annina takes her vows as a nun, becoming Sister Angela.

Meyerbeer, Giacomo. *L'Africaine* (1865)
Librettist: Eugène Scribe
Publishers: Benoit, Garland, Loigerot
214   1. Act III, No. 8, "Choeur de Femmes"
        2. SSAA; Don Pedro (B)
        3. 3 minutes
        4. Medium
        5. A women's chorus aboard Don Pedro's ship describes the floating voyage.
        N.B. Even though the composer lists four women's parts, the chorus never employs more than three voice parts at any given time.

215   1. Act III, No. 9, "Quatuor et Choeur de Matelots"
            2. TTBB; TTBB soli drawn from the chorus
            3. 5 minutes
            4. Moderately Difficult
            5. A quartet and chorus of sailors sings of the
               colors created by the dawn light reflecting off the
               waves.
            N.B. The quartet occasionally doubles the chorus, but
            is usually independent.

216   1. Act III, No. 10, "Prière des Matelots"
            2. SATB divisi; Inez (S), La Suivante (M)
            3. 3.5 minutes
            4. Moderately Difficult
            5. The sailors and women on Don Pedro's ship offer a
               prayer to St. Dominique for protection.
            N.B. The music for Inez and La Suivante is usually
            doubled in the choral parts.

Meyerbeer, Giacomo. *Dinorah* (1859)
Librettists: Jules Barbier and Michel Carré
Publisher: Boosey and Hawkes
217   1. Act I, No. 1, "L'azzuro del ciel"
            2. SATB
            3. 2 minutes
            4. Medium
            5. The opening section of a longer chorus, this portion
               extolls the beauty of a day in the mountains. The
               scene may be extended with parts for two
               goatherds (SA), but those are quite difficult.

218   1. Act II, No. 12, "Come è buon il vin"
            2. SATB; accompaniment *ad libitum*
            3. 2.5 minutes
            4. Medium
            5. A drinking song, sung in anticipation of a holiday
               the next day.

Meyerbeer, Giacomo. *Les Huguenots* (1836)
Librettist: Eugène Scribe, after Deschamps
Publishers: Boosey and Hawkes, Broude Bros., Kalmus,
    Ricordi
219   1. Act I, No. 1b, "Coro"
        2. TTB; TTBB soli drawn from chorus, de Nevers
            (Bar)
        3. 4 minutes
        4. Moderately Difficult
        5. Count de Nevers leads his friends in a toast at a
            banquet in his chateau.

220   1. Act I, No. 1e, "Orgia"
        2. TTBB; Javannes (T), Cossé (T), Retz (Bar), de
            Nevers (Bar), Meru (Bar)
        3. 6 minutes
        4. Difficult
        5. A rousing drinking chorus in praise of Bacchus and
            riotous living.
        N.B. A "chorus of gentlemen" sings short solo phrases
        in small ensembles and also doubles the male chorus.
        These voices may be drawn from the choral forces.

221   1. Act II, No. 8, "Coro e Ballo delle Bagnanti"
        2. SSAA divisi; Marguerite (S), Urbain (M)
        3. 6 minutes
        4. Moderately Difficult
        5. A chorus of women sweetly greets Marguerite and
            sings of the beauty of the day.
        N.B. Urbain's role was originally for soprano and
        requires high sustained singing.

222   1. Act III, No. 15a, "Coro di Soldati Ugnotti"
        2. TTBB divisi; Bois-Rosé (T) and TBB soli
        3. 4 minutes
        4. Difficult
        5. A company of Huguenot soldiers sings a partisan
            chorus in an open place in Paris, before the chapel

where de Nevers is to take Valentine in marriage. The soldiers imitate with their hands the beating of drums.

223   1. Act III, No. 21, "Coro della disputa"
2. SATB divisi
3. 3.5 minutes
4. Moderately Difficult
5. The Catholic and Huguenot women and the Catholic students and Huguenot soldiers engage in a stinging choral dispute, hurling accusations at each other.

224   1. Act IV, No. 24, "Benedizione dei Pugnali"
2. SATB; Monks (TBB), St. Bris (Bar)
3. 8 minutes
4. Difficult
5. A chorus full of religious and vengeful fervor as the Catholics, led by the Count de St. Bris, vow to fight for their cause.

Meyerbeer, Giacomo. *Le Prophète* (1849)
Librettist: Eugène Scribe
Publishers: Broude Bros., Garland, Ricordi, Editions Salabert, G. Schirmer

225   1. Act III, Scene 1, "Ferriam! Ferriam!"
2. SATB
3. 4 minutes
4. Moderately Difficult
5. A chorus that illustrates the contrast of sensuality and piety in the Anabaptists. An opening frenetic dance is briefly interrupted by a phrase from the Te Deum, before continuing.

226   1. Act III, Scene 1, "Son qui le fanciulle del vento"
2. SATB divisi
3. 5.5 minutes

4. Difficult
5. A continuation of the preceding chorus in both
   style and text.

227   1. Act III, Finale, "Münster da lui promessa"
       2. TTBB
       3. 3 minutes
       4. Moderately Difficult
       5. A group of angry soldiers returns to camp
          defeated, about which they angrily sing.

228   1. Act IV, Finale, "Ecco già, il re Profeta"
       2. SATB and children's chorus
       3. 3 minutes
       4. Difficult
       5. John has claimed to be of divine origin, which is
          now challenged by a blind woman who is his
          mother. The chorus reacts as John attempts to
          persuade them that the woman is lying, while he
          knows she is not.

Meyerbeer, Giacomo. *Roberto le Diable* (1831)
Librettists: Eugène Scribe and Casimir Delavigne
Publishers: Boosey and Hawkes, Breitkopf & Härtel, Garland
229   1. Act I, Scene 1, "Choeur des Buveurs"
       2. TTBB; Robert (T), Alberti (B), TTB (Chevaliers)
       3. 5.5 minutes
       4. Moderately Difficult
       5. Robert and Alberti lead a chorus of knights,
          drinking in an effort to forget all care.

Milhaud, Darius. *Christophe Colomb* (1930)
Librettist: Paul Claudel
Publisher: Universal Edition
230   1. Act I, No. 4, "Et la terre était informe"
       2. SATB; S solo

3. 3.5 minutes
4. Difficult
5. This chorus accompanies the image of a spinning globe projected at the back of the stage. The text discusses the spirit of God descending upon the earth.

N.B. This work is often considered as much an oratorio as an opera. The chorus is used extensively throughout the work; given here and below are those scenes which are most easily or appropriately excerpted.

231 1. Act I, No. 12, "Fils de la mer"
2. SATB
3. 3.5 minutes
4. Difficult
5. Taking the role of Columbus, the choir questions a dying sailor to find out what he knows of the sea in the west.

232 1. Act I, No. 16, "C'est vrai que Leurs Majestés"
2. SATB/TTBB dbl. choir; Recruiting Officer and Executioner (speaking roles)
3. 11 minutes
4. Difficult
5. Recruiting is underway in an effort to man the ships sailing under Columbus. A four-part mixed chorus begins the excerpt, later speaking their music; a separate men's chorus portrays the young recruits later in the scene.

233 1. Act I, Finale, "The Redeemer"
2. SATB dbl. choir divisi
3. 4 minutes
4. Difficult
5. A shout of "America!" is heard, followed by a full-throated hymn of thanksgiving upon reaching land.

234   1. Act II, entr'acte, "Ptolemée"
        2. SATB
        3. 4.5 minutes
        4. Difficult
        5. The whole world (literally) is abuzz with the
           excitement surrounding Columbus's discovery.

235   1. Act II, No. 8, "Alleluia"
        2. SATB divisi; Isabella (S)
        3. 8 minutes
        4. Difficult
        5. Isabella, safely ensconced in heaven through the
           help of St. James, leads a prayer for Columbus.

Millöcker, Karl. *Der Bettelstudent* (1882)
Librettists: F. Zell and Richard Genée
Publishers: Boosey and Hawkes, Broude Bros., Chappell;
   Oakland (Calif.) Public Library

236   1. Act I, Nos. 1 and 1b, "Banish grief and care"
        2. SATB
        3. 3.5 minutes
        4. Medium
        5. A group of prisoners' wives has just convinced the
           chief jailer to let them see their husbands. This
           chorus celebrates the granting of that request.
        N.B. The scene may be extended backwards to include
        the opening scene between the wives and the jailer
        (T). Small solo roles with the annotated excerpt are
        doubled in the chorus. This opera was annotated using
        the Boosey and Hawkes score, which is written only in
        English.

237   1. Act I, No. 4, "Hurrah for the fair!"
        2. SAB divisi
        3. 2.5 minutes
        4. Medium

     5. A chorus which enumerates the delights of a
       country fair.

238   1. Act II, Finale, "Here's to you!"
       2. SATB divisi
       3. 4 minutes
       4. Moderately Difficult
       5. A delightful, lively wedding chorus-cum-toast to the
         bride. A solo section in the middle (four very short
         verses, alternating with choral refrains) can easily
         be sung by younger singers of virtually any voice
         range.

Moniusko, Stanislaw. *Halka* (1847)
Librettist: Wlodzimierza Wolskiego (Wolski)
Publishers: Broude Bros., Polish Music Publishers (cw)

239   1. Act I, Scene 5, "Where will you sit, young
         bridegroom?"
       2. TTBB; Janusz (Bar)
       3. 5 minutes
       4. Moderately Difficult
       5. A party is under way celebrating the engagement of
         Zophia, the daughter of a local gentry, to Janusz, a
         young nobleman. This lively chorus precedes a
         dance of the Mazurka.
      N.B. The role of Janusz is short and quite easy in this
      scene and could be sung with little trouble by a young
      baritone.

240   1. Act III, Scene 1, "On the eve of the festival"
       2. SATB (with boy's voices indicated singing the
         soprano part)
       3. 5.5 minutes
       4. Moderately Difficult
       5. Exiting from church, the villagers gossip about
         Janusz's upcoming marriage. After a *moderato*

introduction, the chorus begins to move faster; it resembles a folk song in its melodic contours.

241   1. Act III, Finale, "What a cruel destiny"
2. SATB; Halka (S), Jontek (T), Goral (T)
3. 4.5 minutes
4. Moderately Difficult
5. The squire and his young bride-to-be have been ill-treated at the local manor house. In this chorus, the villagers express their outrage.
N.B. The three principal roles are not difficult.

Montemezzi, Itala. *L'Amore dei tre re* (1913)
Librettist: Sem Benelli
Publishers: Broude Bros., Ricordi
242   1. Act III, Scene 1, "Morte in gelido stupore"
2. SATB divisi; SAT soli drawn from chorus
3. 6.5 minutes
4. Moderately Difficult
5. The peasants of Altura, a remote Italian kingdom, have gathered around the funeral bier of Fiora, daughter-in-law of the King. They express their love for her in this beautiful, lyric dirge.

Monteverdi, Claudio. *L'Incoronazione di Poppea* (1642)
Librettist: Francesco Busenello
Publishers: Broude Bros., Faber, Heugel, Ricordi, Editions Salabert, G. Schirmer, Universal Edition
243   1. Act I, Finale, "Non morir, Seneca"
2. TTB
3. 5.5 minutes
4. Moderately Difficult
5. A moving and passionate chorus. Seneca has called his students together to tell them he will soon be killed. They anxiously – and dramatically – ask him to live.

244   1. Act II, Finale, "A te, sovrana Augusta"
2. TB
3. 4.5 minutes
4. Moderately Difficult
5. The coronation chorus for Poppea, which calls for all nations to honor her. Several sections of this passage might better be sung by soloists.
N.B. The scene may be extended with the addition of two *sinfonie* that precede and follow this chorus.

Monteverdi, Claudio. *L'Orfeo* (1607)
Librettist: Alessandro Striggio
Publishers: Boosey and Hawkes, Broude Bros., J.W. Chester, Costallat, Faber, Gregg, Novello, G. Schirmer, B. Schott's Söhne, Editioni Suvini Zerboni

245   1. Act I, Finale, "Alcun sia che disperato"
2. SATTB
3. 5 minutes
4. Moderately Difficult
5. A duet for two tenors is followed by a three-part trio (SAB) and another duet (AT), and then the five-part chorus, all separated by instrumental *ritornelli*. While the two duets might best be sung by solo voices, the trio and five-part sections are more choral in nature. The text is a pastoral sung by shepherds and nymphs to Orpheus and Euridice, wishing them both happiness.

246   1. Act II, Finale, "Chi ne consola ahi lassi?"
2. SATTB
3. 4 minutes
4. Moderately Difficult
5. Several choral sections separate a series of duets for two tenors, probably intended for solo voices. The excerpt is a lamentation over the fate of both lovers.

247   1. Act III, Finale, "Nulla impresa"
     2. SAATB
     3. 4 minutes
     4. Moderately Difficult
     5. A chorus of spirits sings a delightful madrigal, having been moved by Orpheus's pleadings to return Euridice to him. The spirits wonder who or what could withstand such resolve as the hero shows.

248   1. Act IV, Finale, "E' la virtute un raggio di celeste bellezza"
     2. AATTB
     3. 3 minutes
     4. Moderately Difficult
     5. A somber chorus, in which the spirits bemoan Euridice's fate, which Orpheus won by pleading to Pluto, before losing his lover by his own lack of constancy to her.

Monteverdi, Claudio. *Il Ritorno d'Ulisse in Patria* (1641)
Librettist: Giacomo Badoaro
Publishers: Boosey and Hawkes, Broude Bros., Denkmähler der Tonkunst in Oesterreiche, Faber, Ricordi, B. Schott's Söhne

249   1. Act II, Scene 27, "Giove amoroso"
     2. SATB dbl. choir
     3. 1.5 minutes
     4. Medium
     5. A chorus "in heaven" is answered by a chorus of the gods in this brief Gabrieli-like exchange. A *ritornello* following the excerpt might be added to slightly lengthen the scene.

Moussorgskii, Modest. *Boris Godounov* (1872-4)
Librettist: composer, after Alexander Pushkin
Publishers: Broude Bros., Kalmus, Oxford, G. Schirmer
250　1. Prologue, Scene 1, "Glory to the Most High be
　　　　given"
　　　2. SATB divisi
　　　3. 3 minutes
　　　4. Moderately Difficult
　　　5. The famous Pilgrim's Chorus, sung as the pilgrims
　　　　make their way to the monastery of Novodevichy.

251　1. Act III, Scene 1, "By the Wisla's blue waters"
　　　2. SSAA
　　　3. 3.5 minutes
　　　4. Medium
　　　5. A group of young girls in Marina's room sings this
　　　　folksong-like chorus about love, while Marina does
　　　　her toilette.
　　　N.B. A short line by Marina may be omitted.

252　1. Act IV, Scene 1, "Lead him this way!"
　　　2. SATB
　　　3. 6 minutes
　　　4. Moderately Difficult
　　　5. The peasants have captured the boyar Khroustshov
　　　　in chains; they bait and mock him, and the false
　　　　tsar Boris, as well. Many parts of this chorus are
　　　　written only for men's or women's voices.

Moussorgskii, Modest. *The Khovansky Rising* or *The Princes
Khovansky* (*Khovanschchina*)
Librettists: composer and Vladimir V. Stassov
Publishers: Breitkopf & Härtel, Kalmus, G. Schirmer
253　1. Act III, Scene 1, "We have conquered"
　　　2. TBB
　　　3. 2.5 minutes
　　　4. Medium

> 5. Sung by a chorus of Old Believers, who act in
> concert with Prince Khovansky who is trying to
> usurp the Tsar's throne. In this scene, the Old
> Believers march through Streltzy's Square, near
> the Kremlin, singing that they have overcome evil
> and triumphed over their enemies.

254   1. Act III, Scene 6, "Get up you lazy men!"
       2. TTBB
       3. 3.5 minutes
       4. Medium
       5. A group of Streltzy (guards) rouses themselves from
          sleep and prepares for an upcoming battle,
          bolstering their courage with drink.

N.B. The scene might be slightly extended by including
the following music where the wives rush in to upbraid
their husbands; however, the ending is not quite
satisfactory. In the annotated portion of this scene, a
solo part for Shaklovity is short and may be omitted.

Moussorgskii, Modest. *Sorotchinsky Fair* (*Sorochinskaya
   Yarmaka*)
Librettist: composer, after Nikolai Gogol
Publishers: Josef Bessel, Broude Bros., Kalmus, G. Schirmer
255   1. Act II, Finale, "Ha! ha! ha!"
       2. SATB dbl. choir
       3. 3 minutes
       4. Difficult
       5. A laughing chorus, consisting of only the title words
          and "tra-la-la," sung after a boy has been revealed
          hiding in the ceiling.

N.B. Unfinished at the composer's death, this opera
was completed by M.N. Tcherepnine.

256   1. Act III, Finale, "The Hopak!"
       2. SATB
       3. 6 minutes

4. Moderately Difficult
5. A joyous chorus, urging all to dance the *hopak*,
   in celebration of the coming wedding of two
   peasants.

Mozart, Wolfgang Amadeus. *La Clemenza di Tito* (1791)
Librettist: Caterino Mazzolà, after Pietro Metastasio
Publishers: Bärenreiter, Breitkopf & Härtel, Broude Bros.,
   Kalmus, International, B. Schott's Söhne

257　1. Act I, Scene 4, "Serbate, O Dei custodi"
2. SATB
3. 2 minutes
4. Medium
5. A chorus sung to the gods asking to preserve Titus.
   N.B. This chorus is repeated after an intervening
   recitative.

258　1. Act II, Scene 4, "Ah grazie si rendano"
2. SATB; Tito (T)
3. 2.5 minutes
4. Medium
5. A choral prayer thanking the Guardian Diety of
   Rome who, through Titus, has preserved the
   splendor of her throne.

259　1. Act II, Scene 15, "Che del ciel, che degli Dei"
2. SATB
3. 4 minutes
4. Easy
5. The crowd praises the Emperor, but wonders why
   he takes no joy knowing he is in the protection of
   the gods.

Mozart, Wolfgang Amadeus. *Così fan tutte* (1790)
Librettist: Lorenzo da Ponte
Publishers: Bärenreiter, Boosey and Hawkes, Broude Bros.,
   Eulenberg, Dover, Jerona, Kalmus, Ricordi, G. Schirmer

260   1. Act I, No. 8, "Bella vita militar"
         2. SATB
         3. 2.5 minutes
         4. Medium
         5. The soldiers and villagers greet an approaching
            barge with an exuberant chorus full of military
            fervor.
         N.B. This chorus is repeated after the following
         recitative and quintet; the opera also has several other
         very short choral segments.

Mozart, Wolfgang Amadeus. *Don Giovanni* (1787)
Librettist: Lorenzo da Ponte
Publishers: Bärenreiter, Boosey and Hawkes, Broude Bros.,
   Dover, Eulenberg, International, Jerona, Kalmus, Ricordi,
   G. Schirmer
261   1. Act I, No. 5, "Giovinette, che fate all'amore"
         2. SATB; Zerlina (S), Masetto (B)
         3. 2.5 minutes
         4. Medium
         5. The villagers dance and sing joyfully
            around the young couple.

Mozart, Wolgang Amadeus. *Die Entführung aus dem Serail*
   (1782)
Librettist: Gottlieb Stephanie, after Bretzner
Publishers: Bärenreiter, Boosey and Hawkes, Broude Bros.,
   Dover, Eulenberg, International, Jerona, Kalmus
262   1. Act I, No. 5, "Singt dem grossen Bassa Lieher"
         2. SATB
         3. 3 minutes
         4. Moderately Difficult
         5. A joyful chorus in praise of the mighty Pasha.
         N.B. The middle section of this chorus specifies solo
         voices, but might be done using either full or semi-
         chorus.

263   1. Act III, No. 21, "Bassa Selim lange"
       2. SATB
       3. 2.5 minutes
       4. Medium
       5. Another chorus in praise of the Pasha; similar
          in style and mood to the previous chorus.

Mozart, Wolfgang Amadeus. *Idomeneo* (1781)
Librettist: Abbé Varesco, after Campra and Danchet
Publishers: Bärenreiter, Boosey and Hawkes, Broude Bros.,
    International, Kalmus

264   1. Act I, No. 3, "Godiam la pace"
       2. SATB; 2 solo Cretes (SA) and 2 solo Trojans (TB)
       3. 3 minutes
       4. Easy
       5. A chorus of Trojans and Cretes rejoices at the news
          of the release of the Trojan prisoners.
       N.B. The solo passages could easily be sung by
       sections of the choir.

265   1. Act I, No. 5, "Pietà Numi, pietà"
       2. TTBB dbl. choir
       3. 4 minutes
       4. Moderately Difficult
       5. A chorus of intercession sung on behalf of Elettra
          by a double men's choir. One chorus is nearby and
          the other is sung in the distance.

266   1. Intermezzo, No. 9, "Nettune s'onori, quel nome
          risuoni"
       2. SATB; SATB soli
       3. 9 minutes
       4. Medium
       5. A lovely choral *ciaccona* in honor of Neptune.
       N.B. The solo passages are extensive and are more
       difficult than the choral portions.

267   1. Act II, No. 17, "Qual nuova terrore!"
        2. SATB
        3. 2 minutes
        4. Medium
        5. The chorus heralds the storm beginning in the
           harbor that signals Neptune's vengeance.
        N.B. The soprano part has a high tessitura.

268   1. Act II, No. 18, "Corriamo, fuggiamo quel mostro
           spietato!"
        2. SATB
        3. 3 minutes
        4. Moderately Difficult
        5. The storm continues and the crowd flees in terror.

269   1. Act III, No. 24, "Oh, oh voto tremenda!"
        2. SATB; Gran Sacerdote (T)
        3. 3.5 minutes
        4. Moderately Difficult
        5. The High Priest and the chorus plead with the King
           to confess his sins to Neptune. The people are
           shocked at hearing that Idamante will be sacrificed
           to appease the god.

270   1. Act III, No. 31, "Scenda amor"
        2. SATB
        3. 4 minutes
        4. Medium
        5. The people celebrate the accession of Idamante to
           the throne.

Mozart, Wolfgang Amadeus. *Le nozze di Figaro* (1786)
Librettist: Lorenzo da Ponte
Publishers: Bärenreiter, Boosey and Hawkes, Broude Bros.,
    Dover, International, Jerona, Ricordi, G. Schirmer
271   1. Act I, No. 8, "Giovanni liete"
        2. SATB

3. 1.5 minutes
4. Medium
5. A delightful chorus of countrymen and women who spread flowers from baskets as they sing for the Count.
N.B. This chorus is repeated after an intervening recitative.

272   1. Act III, Finale, "Amanti costanti segnaci"
2. SATB
3. 1.5 minutes
4. Medium
5. A chorus celebrating a double wedding.
N.B. The Finale also contains other short choral excerpts and a lovely duet for two young girls, which could easily be fashioned into a usable choral excerpt.

Mozart, Wolfgang Amadeus. *Die Zauberflöte* (1791)
Librettist: Emmanuel Schikaneder
Publishers: Bärenreiter, Boosey and Hawkes, Broude Bros., Dover, Eulenberg, Jerona, Ricordi, G. Schirmer

273   1. Act I, Finale, "Es lebe Sarastro!"
2. SATB; Pamina (S), Papageno (Bar)
3. 2.5 minutes
4. Medium
5. An offstage chorus praises Sarastro. The sentiments of the chorus as well as the sight of the approaching Sarastro terrorize Pamina and Papageno.

274   1. Act I, Finale, "Wenn Tugend und Gerechtigkeit"
2. SATB
3. 1.5 minutes
4. Medium
5. This chorus is sung while Tamino and Papageno are being brought to the temple for the purification ritual.

N.B. Although the excerpt is straightforward, the choral parts require a rather high tessitura.

275   1. Act II, No. 18, "O Isis und Osiris, welche Wonne!"
       2. TTB
       3. 4 minutes
       4. Moderately Difficult
       5. A chorus of priests sings prayerfully in thankfulness to the gods.

276   1. Act II, Finale, "Heil sei euch Geweihten!" and "Es siegte die Stärke"
       2. SATB
       3. 2.5 minutes
       4. Moderately Difficult
       5. The choral Finale to the opera is in two parts: the first an *andante* prayer to Osiris and Isis, and the second an *allegro* victory chorus.

N

Nicolai, Otto. *Lustigen Weiber von Windsor* (1849)
Librettist: Hermann von Mosenthal, after William Shakespeare
Publishers:Broude Bros., Kalmus, Ricordi, G. Schirmer
277   1. Act III, Scene 5, "O süsser Mond"
       2. SATB divisi
       3. 2 minutes
       4. Medium
       5. A magical chorus, sung in Windsor Forest at night.

278   1. Act III, Scene 9, "Ihr Elfen, Weiss und Rot und Grau"
       2. SSAA

3. 1.5 minutes
4. Moderately Difficult
5. A delightful chorus sung by elves and spirits in
   the woods.

279 1. Act III, Scene 13, "Mücken, Wespen, Fliegenchor"
    2. SATB; Spärlich (T), Reich (B), Falstaff (B), Dr.
       Cajus (B)
    3. 2.5 minutes
    4. Medium
    5. A novelty chorus of insects tormenting Falstaff; the
       other principals, in disguise, join in the fun.

280 1. Act III, Scene 14, "Fasst ihn, Geister"
    2. SATTB
    3. 3.5 minutes
    4. Moderately Difficult
    5. The full chorus, in masks and costumed as spirits,
       rushes in and torments Falstaff in all variety of
       manners.

Nielsen, Carl. *Masquerade* (*Maskarade*) (1906)
Librettist: Vilhelm Andersen, after Ludvig Holberg
Publisher: Wilhelm Hansen Musik Verlag
281 1. Act III, "Kehrano! Kehrano! Dance on!"
    2. SATB; Henry (Bar)
    3. 4 minutes
    4. Medium
    5. After all masquerades have been dropped, a joyful
       final chorus is sung, full of dancing and
       celebration.
    N.B. Other characters double the choral parts in the
    final portion of this excerpt.

Nielsen, Carl. *Saul and David* (1902)
Librettist: Ejnar Christiansen
Publishers: Broude Bros., J.W. Chester, Wilhelm Hansen
  Musik Forlag

282   1. Act I, "God be our shield and fortress"
       2. SATB divisi
       3. 3.5 minutes
       4. Moderately Difficult
       5. The priests and the people sing a reverent choral
          prayer as they await the coming of Samuel.
       N.B. There are segments of this chorus scored for just
       men's or women's voices.

283   1. Act II, "Hallelujah!"
       2. SATB divisi; Saul (Bar)
       3. 7.5 minutes
       4. Moderately Difficult
       5. The crowd sings a chorus of thanksgiving at the
          return of the Israelite soldiers, led by David and
          Saul. The King proceeds to give Mikal to David in
          marriage.

284   1. Act III, "God is our witness"
       2. SATB divisi; Mikal (S), Saul (Bar)
       3. 8 minutes
       4. Moderately Difficult
       5. In Saul's camp, the people witness David re-affirm
          his loyalty to Saul. They sing a lengthy and
          inventive fugal chorus.

285   1. Act IV, "In thee now is Israel's hope"
       2. SATB divisi; David (T)
       3. 6 minutes
       4. Moderately Difficult
       5. In a grand and noble chorus on Mount Gilboa, the
          people proclaim David their king.

O

Offenbach, Jacques. *La Belle Hélène* (1864)
Librettists: Henri Meilhac and Ludovic Halévy
Publishers: Broude Bros., Heugel, G. Schirmer
286   1. Act I, No. 1, "Vers tes autels"
      2. SATTB; 2 young women (SS)
      3. 3.5 minutes
      4. Medium
      5. A chorus mockingly pays tribute to Jupiter during a
         festival in honor of Venus.

287   1. Act I, No. 7, "Voici les Rois"
      2. SATB divisi
      3. 2 minutes
      4. Medium
      5. A comic choral march.
      N.B. There is a short reprise of this march later in the
      same scene.

288   1. Act III, No. 18, "Dansons!"
      2. SATB divisi
      3. 3 minutes
      4. Medium
      5. The Spartans joyfully sing praise to Venus and
         Bacchus.

Offenbach, Jacques. *Les Contes d'Hoffmann* (1881)
Librettists: Jules Barbier and Michel Carré
Publishers: Broude Bros., Kalmus, G. Schirmer
289   1. Act I, No. 1, "Drig, drig, drig, maître Luther"
      2. TTBB; Nathanaël (T), Hermann (B), Luther (B)
      3. 3 minutes
      4. Moderately Difficult
      5. A lively drinking chorus in Luther's tavern in
         Nürnberg.

290 1. Act II, No. 6, "Non, aucun hôte, vraiment"
2. SATTB
3. 2 minutes
4. Medium
5. In a choral minuet, the guests thank their host
Spalanzani for his hospitality.
N.B. The remainder of the act has many fine short
choral and ensemble passages.

Offenbach, Jacques. *Orphée aux Enfers* (1858)
Librettists: Hector Crémieux and Ludovic Halévy
Publishers: Broude Bros., Heugel, Kalmus, G. Schirmer, Josef
Weinberger
291 1. Act I, No. 1, "Voici la douzième heure"
2. SATBB
3. 4 minutes
4. Easy
5. The shepherds and shepherdesses sing a
pastoral.
N.B. There is a short instrumental prelude to the
chorus, a middle section with dialogue, and then a
reprise of the chorus.

292 1. Act I, No. 7, "Viens! c'est l'honneur"
2. SATB divisi; Calliope (M), Orpheus (T)
3. 3 minutes
4. Moderately Difficult
5. In this delightful Finale of Act I, Orpheus complains
about his treatment in the underworld; Calliope
(Public Opinion) encourages him, and the chorus
adds their support.

293 1. Act II, No. 16, "Gloire à Jupiter"
2. SATB divisi; SATB soli
3. 2 minutes
4. Medium

5. The gods and goddesses decide to *all* go to Hades
   to look for Eurydice in a lively *galop* chorus.
   N.B. The entire Act II Finale employs chorus; this
   excerpt is the final section, and requires a short
   passage to be sung by a group of principals; sections of
   the chorus are repeated as part of the final curtain
   call.

294
1. Act IV, No. 22, "Vive le vin!"
2. SATB divisi
3. 2 minutes
4. Medium
5. A rousing *choeur infernal* sung by the chorus with
   Venus and Cupid (whose lines are doubled in the
   choral parts).

295
1. Act IV, No. 28, "Menuet"
2. SATB divisi; Jupiter (Bar), Pluto (Bar)
3. 2.5 minutes
4. Moderately Difficult
5. Jupiter suggests dancing a minuet and the chorus
   comments on his abilities.

296
1. Act IV, No. 28, "Galop infernal"
2. SATB divisi
3. 2 minutes
4. Medium
5. The well-known can-can tune, perhaps the most
   famous piece from this opera, is sung by the
   chorus mostly on neutral vowel syllables.

Offenbach, Jacques. *La Périchole* (1868)
Librettists: Henri Meilhac and Ludovic Halévy, after Prosper
  Mérimée
Publishers: Boosey and Hawkes, Broude Bros., Kalmus, G.
  Schirmer

297   1. Act I, No. 1, "Du Vice-Roy, c'est aujord' hui la fête"
       2. SATTB
       3. 2 minutes
       4. Medium
       5. Set on the public square in Lima, Peru, in front of
          the café of the "Three Cousins," the opera opens
          with this lively drinking chorus.

298   1. Act II, Finale, "Nous allons donc voir un mari"
       2. SATB divisi; Viceroy (Bar), Pedro (Bar)
       3. 2.5 minutes
       4. Medium
       5. The chorus takes great delight in the introduction of
          the Countess to the Viceroy.

299   1. Act III, No. 18, "En avant soldats"
       2. TB; Pedro (Bar)
       3. 5 minutes
       4. Medium
       5. The soldiers and Pedro are marching about the
          public square searching for the runaways (who are
          hiding in the café).

P

Penderecki, Krysztof. *Die Teufen von Loudon* (*The Devils of
    Loudun*) (1969)
Librettist: composer, after Whiting and Aldous Huxley
Publisher: B. Schott's Söhne
300   1. Act III, Scene 7, "Juste judex"
       2. SATB 16-part divisi
       3. 4 minutes
       4. Difficult

5. A procession carrying Grandier on a litter moves past St. Peter's Church and on to St. Ursula's convent. The chorus intones multiple texts in Latin. When Grandier attempts to speak, the noise from the crowd drowns him out.

N.B. As one might expect, Penderecki's score is highly complex, and the chorus is asked to perform difficult musical and vocal effects. Near the end of the opera, there are similar passages to that annotated here, but not as easy to excerpt.

Pepusch, John Christopher. *The Beggar's Opera* (1728)
Librettist: John Gay
Publisher: Boosey and Hawkes
301   1. Act II, Nos. 19-20, "Fill every glass"
     2. TBB divisi; Filch (T)
     3. 2.5 minutes
     4. Medium
     5. Filch and the gang sing a drinking song in a tavern near Newgate.

N.B. This opera exists in several different versions. These excerpts were annotated using the Boosey and Hawkes score.

302   1. Act II, No. 21, "Let us take the road"
     2. TBB; Filch (T)
     3. 2 minutes
     4. Medium
     5. Filch and the gang leave the tavern singing this short chorus to the melody of a march from Handel's *Rinaldo*. The last line of the text reads: "T' your arms brave boys and load, see the ball I hold! Let chemists toil like asses. . ."

303   1. Act II, No. 24, "Youth's the season"
     2. SA; Macheath (T)
     3. 2 minutes

4. Easy

5. As the women arrive at the tavern after an invitation from Macheath, he leads them in a merry song and dance.

N.B. The role of Macheath is written for a low tenor.

304   1. Act III, No. 40, "In a humour I was of late"

2. SATB; T solo

3. 2 minutes

4. Medium

5. In a gaming house, the men and women assembled muse on the joys of drinking.

305   1. Act III, No. 41, "The modes of the court so common are grown"

2. SATB; Macheath (T), Filch (T)

3. 3 minutes

4. Medium

5. Macheath, Filch, and the chorus sing and whistle this memorable chorus, based on the tune "Lillibulero."

306   1. Act III, No. 54, "Thus I stand like the Turk"

2. SATB; Macheath (T), several short soli

3. 3 minutes

4. Moderately Difficult

5. The opera's Finale contains its moral: "The wretch of today may be happy tomorrow." The passage is unusual in its double chorus effect, with the principals singing "ah" and the chorus singing the more important musical material.

Pfitzner, Hans. *Palestrina* (1917)

Librettist: composer

Publishers: Broude Bros., Fürstner, G. Schirmer, B. Schott's Söhne

307 1. Act II, "Die Italiener dort seht!"
2. TTBB; Graf Luna (Bar)
3. 4 minutes
4. Difficult
5. The Council of Trent is meeting at the palace of
   Cardinal Madruscht, and all of the delegates are
   suspicious of each other. In this chorus the
   Spaniards comment on the Italians who are
   "swarming all over like ants."

N.B. As might be expected, an opera about Palestrina
contains many choral excerpts. Most of the choruses
here are too short to excerpt: those looking for a
particularly interesting scene may be interested in one
where a Mass is dictated to the composer by a chorus
of angels.

308 1. Act III, Scene 2, "Ist Palestrina, der Meister, hier?"
2. TTBB dbl. choir
3. 2 minutes
4. Difficult
5. The singers from the papal chapel are asking to see
   the master, Palestrina. They bring the news that
   the Pope has proclaimed the Mass composition
   the composer's best work.

Ponchielli, Amilcare. *La Gioconda* (1876)
Librettist: Arrigo Boito
Publishers: Broude Bros., International, Kalmus, Ricordi, G.
  Schirmer
309 1. Act I, "Feste! Pane!"
2. SATB divisi; Barnaba (Bar)
3. 3.5 minutes
4. Moderately Difficult
5. A large crowd of monks, sailors, and other merrymakers fills the stage, singing about sports and
   feasting. When Barnaba announces the approaching Regatta, the people leave to watch.

310   1. Act I, "Gloria a chi vince"
2. SATB divisi
3. 2 minutes
4. Moderately Difficult
5. When the Regatta is over, the crowd returns singing
the praises of the victor.

311   1. Act I, "Angele Dei"
2. SATB divisi; Gioconda (S), La Cieca (A), Un
Barnabotta (Bar)
3. 6 minutes
4. Difficult
5. A *barnabotta* (monk) and the chorus chant in the
church while Gioconda is dismayed that Enzo has
forsaken her. La Cieca comforts her.
N.B. There are several unaccompanied passages for
the chorus.

312   1. Act III, "La gaia canzone"
2. SATB divisi; Gioconda (S), Laura (M), Alvise (B)
3. 4 minutes
4. Moderately Difficult
5. A gay serenade is sung offstage by the chorus in
gondolas in the canal, and provides the musical
background for intrigue involving poison and
deceit onstage.

313   1. Act III, Scene 6, "S'inneggi alla Cà d'Oro"
2. SATB divisi
3. 1.5 minutes
4. Moderately Difficult
5. A festive scene in Alvise's house where the host is
receiving his guests.

Poulenc, Francis. *Dialogues des Carmélites* (1955)
Librettist: Georges Bernanos
Publishers: Broude Bros., Ricordi, G. Schirmer

314   1. Act II, Scene 2, "Ave Maria"
2. SSA; La Prieure (S), Mère Marie (S)
3. 1.5 minutes
4. Moderately Difficult
5. The nuns sing a haunting setting of the prayerful
text.

315   1. Act III, Scene 4, "Salve Regina"
2. SATB divisi/SSAA dbl. choir; Blanche (S)
3. 10 minutes
4. Difficult
5. The chilling last scene of the opera uses both a
mixed chorus on neutral vowel syllables and a
nun's chorus singing the hymn tune. The score is
punctuated at irregular intervals with the sound of
the guillotine, as the nuns are executed one by
one.
N.B. The nun's chorus obviously decreases in size as
the scene unfolds, leaving only Blanche to sing the
final few phrases.

Prokofiev, Serge. *Betrothal in a Monastery* (*La Duenna*) (1946)
Librettist: Mira Mendelson, after Sheridan
Publisher: Leeds (cw); OSU
316   1. Act II, "Fishwives' Chorus"
2. SSA
3. 2 minutes
4. Difficult
5. At the waterfront, fishwives sell their products with
verve.

Prokofiev, Serge. *The Gambler* (*Igrok*) (1928)
Librettist: composer, after Fyodor Dostoevsky
Publishers: Boosey and Hawkes, Broude Bros., Leeds (cw),
Moscow State Music Publishers, G. Schirmer

317   1. Act III, Scene 2, "Only a hundred thousand francs"
       2. SATB divisi
       3. 7 minutes
       4. Difficult
       5. The chorus can't believe Alexis's good luck when
          he gambles and breaks the bank. In the opera,
          sung in front of the curtain.

Prokofiev, Serge. *The Love for Three Oranges* (*Lyubov k trem
    Apelsinam*) (1921)
Librettist: composer, after Gozzi
Publishers: Boosey and Hawkes, Broude Bros., Leeds (cw), G.
    Schirmer
318   1. Prologue, "The Dispute"
       2. SATB divisi/SB dbl. choir
       3. 2.5 minutes
       4. Difficult
       5. The prologue of the opera presents various groups
          of entertainers, each supporting their own
          particular interests. The tragedians, the comics, the
          lyrics and the empty heads all vie for center stage.

Prokofiev, Serge. *War and Peace* (*Voina y Mir*) (1945)
Librettists: composer and Mira Mendelson, after Leo Tolstoy
Publishers: Broude Bros., Kalmus, G. Schirmer
319   1. Part I, "The Epigraph"
       2. SATB divisi
       3. 8 minutes
       4. Moderately Difficult
       5. This massive homophonic chorus begins the opera.
          The excerpt symbolizes the strengths of Russia in
          the face of her detractors.

320   1. Part II, Scene 8, "Working Song"
       2. TTBB/SSATTB dbl. choir
       3. 3.5 minutes

4. Difficult
5. The men's chorus, and later a mixed chorus, sings a
   fervent working song.
N.B. There are several similar, but shorter choruses in
the same scene.

321   1. Part II, Scene 11, "Muscovites' Chorus"
      2. SATTB
      3. 4 minutes
      4. Difficult
      5. A crowd of frenzied Muscovites sets fire to their
         city rather than surrender it.

322   1. Part II, Scene 13, "Choruses to the Russian Spirit"
      2. SATB divisi
      3. 20 minutes
      4. Moderately Difficult to Difficult
      5. These four grand patriotic choruses end the opera;
         the choruses begin at rehearsal numbers 538, 540,
         550, and 555.

Puccini, Giacomo. *La Bohème* (1896)
Librettists: Giuseppe Giacosa and Luigi Illica
Publishers: Broude Bros., Dover, Kalmus, Ricordi, G.
   Schirmer
323   1. Act II, Finale, "Ecco il tambur maggiore!"
      2. SATB divisi, children's chorus; Mimi (S), Musetta
         (S), Rodolfo (T), Marcello (Bar), Schaunard
         (Bar), Colline (B)
      3. 1.5 minutes
      4. Moderately Difficult
      5. The rousing Finale to the highly complex second act
         of the opera. All of the various townspeople,
         vendors, and street urchins join the choral march.
         The principals' singing is incidental and at the end,
         doubles the choral parts.

Puccini, Giacomo. *Madama Butterfly* (1904)
Librettists: Giuseppe Giacosa and Luigi Illica
Publishers: Broude Bros., Dover, Kalmus, Ricordi, G.
  Schirmer
324   1. Act I, "Quanto cielo! quanto mar!"
        2. SSA; Butterfly (S), Sharpless (Bar)
        3. 2 minutes
        4. Medium
        5. Butterfly and her relatives and friends arrive at a
             small house on the hill that Pinkerton has leased
             for them.
        N.B. Butterfly's singing is much more difficult than the
        chorus's.

325   1. Act II, "Humming Chorus"
        2. ST
        3. 2.5 minutes
        4. Moderately Difficult
        5. An exquisite offstage humming chorus, sung while
             Butterfly, her little son, and Suzuki await
             Pinkerton's return.

Puccini, Giacomo. *Manon Lescaut* (1893)
Librettists: M. Praga, D. Oliva, Luigi Illica, and G. Ricordi
Publishers: Broude Bros., Kalmus, Ricordi, G. Schirmer
326   1. Act I, "Giovinezza è il nostro nome"
        2. SATB divisi; Edmondo (T)
        3. 2 minutes
        4. Moderately Difficult
        5. In front of the inn at Amiens, a scene of great joy
             and activity is unfolding. Edmondo sings a solo
             about youth and gladness which is then echoed by
             the students and girls.

327   1. Act I, "Ma bravo!"
        2. SATB divisi
        3. 2 minutes

4. Difficult

5. After the assembled crowd has teased Des Grieux and he has responded, a joyful chorus ensues.

328   1. Act II, "Sulla vetta tu del monte erri, o Clori"

2. SSAA; M solo

3. 2 minutes

4. Moderately Difficult

5. A group of women sings a madrigal composed by Geronte for Manon.

Puccini, Giacomo. *La Rondine* (1917)

Librettist: Giuseppe Adami, after Willner and Reichert

Publishers: Broude Bros., Universal Edition

329   1. Act II, "Fiori freschi"

2. SATB divisi; several short incidental soli

3. 2 minutes

4. Difficult

5. This chorus is very similar in mood to the second act of *La Bohème*. The act opens with a very busy chorus of students, grisettes, customers, waiters, and flower girls. The scene is wonderfully active and confusing.

N.B. There are a number of ways to satisfactorily conclude this excerpt, from which the performer will need to choose.

330   1. Act II, "Vuoi tu dirmi che cosa"

2. SATB divisi

3. 1.5 minutes

4. Moderately Difficult

5. A charming waltz chorus sung between lovers.

N.B. The scene may be extended by including the ensuing dance, following which the music annotated above is reprised by the chorus and principals.

Puccini, Giacomo. *Suor Angelica* (1918)
Librettist: Giovacchino Forzano
Publishers: Broude Bros., Kalmus, Ricordi, G. Schirmer
331   1. "O Madonna, salvami!"
         2. SATB divisi; Suor Angelica (S)
         3. 4 minutes
         4. Difficult
         5. At the end of the opera, Sister Angelica decides to
            commit suicide. As she takes her own life, she
            prays to the Virgin that she may not die in mortal
            sin. An offstage chorus of nuns, children, and
            others sings to the Madonna.

Puccini, Giacomo. *Tosca* (1900)
Librettists: Giuseppe Giacosa and Luigi Illica, after Victorien
   Sardou
Publishers: Broude Bros., Kalmus, Ricordi, G. Schirmer
332   1. Act II, "Sale, ascendi l'uman cantico"
         2. SATB divisi; Tosca (S), Cavaradossi (T), Spoletta
            (T), Scarpia (Bar)
         3. 3.5 minutes
         4. Difficult
         5. A beautiful cantata, led by Tosca, emanates from
            the Queen's reception rooms. While the cantata
            proceeds, a scene between Scarpia, Cavaradossi
            and Spoletta unfolds simultaneously.

Puccini, Giacomo. *Turandot* (1926)
Librettists: Giuseppe Adami and R. Simoni, after Gozzi
Publishers: Broude Bros., Ricordi, G. Schirmer
333   1. Act I, "Gira la cote"
         2. SATB divisi
         3. 5.5 minutes
         4. Difficult
         5. The crowd outside the Imperial Palace is eagerly
            awaiting an execution. They urge the executioner

to sharpen his ceremonial sword and they await
the rising of the moon, the sign for the execution
to begin.
N.B. A solo group of executioner's assistants (basses)
sings throughout the excerpt.

334 1. Act I, "Perchè tarda la luna?"
2. SATB divisi, children's chorus in unison
3. 7 minutes
4. Moderately Difficult
5. The crowd watches the sky, anxiously awaiting the
rising of the moon which will signal the time for
the execution. Tardy, the moon eventually appears.

335 1. Act II, Scene 2, "Ai tuoi piedi ci prostriam"
2. SATB divisi
3. 2.5 minutes
4. Moderately Difficult
5. The Prince ascends the stairs as the Imperial hymn,
accompanied by onstage brass and organ, is sung
again.

Purcell, Henry. *Dido and Aeneas* (1689)
Librettist: Nahum Tate
Publishers: Broude Bros., Novello
336 1. Act I, No. 7, "Fear no danger to ensue"
2. SATB divisi; Belinda (S), Second Woman (S)
3. 2.5 minutes
4. Medium
5. The chorus takes up and develops the lovely duet
between Belinda and the Second Woman, urging
Dido to "fear no danger."
N.B. This opera is full of very short choruses that
might be excerpted and easily grouped in performance.

337 1. Act I, No. 12, "To the hills and the vales"
2. SATB

3. 1.5 minutes
4. Medium
5. A chorus of triumph and joy, followed in the score
  by a "triumphing dance."

338   1. Act II, No. 24, "Thanks to these lonesome,
    lonesome vales"
2. SATB; Belinda (S)
3. 3 minutes
4. Medium
5. The chorus continues Belinda's lovely melody; sung
  in the woods.

339   1. Act III, No. 29, "Come away, fellow sailors"
2. SATB; First Sailor (T)
3. 1.5 minutes
4. Medium
5. The sailors sing of their intention to go to sea and
  not return.
N.B. The scene may be extended by the inclusion of
the charming instrumental prelude and the sailors'
dance which surround this excerpt.

340   1. Act III, No. 39, "With drooping wings"
2. SATB
3. 2 minutes
4. Medium
5. The touching last chorus of the opera, sung by
  hovering Cupids.

R

Ravel, Maurice. *L'Enfant et les Sortilèges* (1925)
Librettist: Collete
Publishers: Broude Bros., Durand, G. Schirmer
341   1. "Adieu, pastourelles"
      2. SATB divisi; Une Pastourelle (S), Un Pâtre (A)
      3. 3.5 minutes
      4. Difficult
      5. After the Child has wreaked his havoc, there is a procession of shepherds and shepherdesses from the destroyed wallpaper, who sing this half-comic, half-serious chorus.

342   1. "Ah! C'est l'Enfant au couteau!"
      2. SATB divisi; Une Chonette (S), several incidental soli
      3. 5.5 minutes
      4. Difficult
      5. The animals begin to torment the Child, but their attitudes change as they observe him binding a squirrel's wound.

343   1. "Il est bon, l'Enfant"
      2. SATB divisi; l'Enfant (M)
      3. 3 minutes
      4. Moderately Difficult
      5. As the opera ends, the animals sing this stirring chorus as they lead the Child back to his house.

Rimsky-Korsakov, Nicolai. *The Golden Cockerell* (*Le Coq d'Or*) (1909)
Librettist: V. Bielsky, after Alexander Pushkin
Publishers: Elkan-Vogel, Kalmus
344   1. Act I, No. 2, "We gather here"
      2. SATB divisi

     3. 2 minutes
     4. Medium
     5. At the court of King Dodon, the courtiers await His
        Majesty's entrance.

345   1. Act I, No. 6, "Lullaby"
     2. SA
     3. 2 minutes
     4. Easy
     5. As the women sing this charming lullaby, the entire
        court, including the King, falls asleep.

346   1. Act II, No. 4, and Act III, No. 1, "March"
     2. SATB divisi
     3. 2 minutes (total)
     4. Medium
     5. Act II ends and Act III begins with the same choral
        march using two different texts.
     N.B. The bass part, in the Russian tradition, is very
     low.

Rimsky-Korsakov, Nicolai. **May Night** (*Mayskaya noch*) (1880)
Librettist: composer, after Nicolai Gogol
Publishers: Belaieff (Leipzig), Kalmus; LC
347   1. Act I, No. 1, "Harvest Chorus"
     2. SATB dbl. choir
     3. 6.5 minutes
     4. Moderately Difficult
     5. The peasants celebrate Whitsuntide with games and
        dances. The two choirs sing in a choral dialogue
        and each choir carries a segment of the selection
        alone.

348   1. Act I, No. 8, "Song of the Village Mayor"
     2. TTBB; Levko (T)
     3. 3 minutes

   4. Moderately Difficult
   5. Levko leads the men of the village in a lively song, mocking the Mayor outside his house.

349 1. Act III, No. 13b, "Chorus of Nixens"
     2. SSAA divisi; Levko (T)
     3. 6 minutes
     4. Moderately Difficult
     5. A lilting 6/8 chorus sung by water nymphs.

Rimsky-Korsakov, Nicolai. *Sadko* (1898)
Librettists: composer and V.I. Bielsky
Publishers: Boosey and Hawkes, Kalmus
350 1. Tableau I, "Merchants' Chorus"
     2. TTBB divisi
     3. 9 minutes
     4. Difficult
     5. The merchants of Novgorod feast as they sing this lengthy, rousing chorus that celebrates their good fortune.

351 1. Tableau I, "Bravo, good Sadko"
     2. TB divisi
     3. 3.5 minutes
     4. Difficult
     5. The feast continues and the merchants laud Sadko.

352 1. Tableau I, "Songs and Dances"
     2. SATTBB; MMTB soli
     3. 5.5 minutes
     4. Difficult
     5. Numerous dances and choruses, sung by the assembled merchants and buffoons, end the tableau with a flourish.

353 1. Tableau VI, "Wedding Chorus"
     2. SATB divisi

3. 4 minutes
4. Difficult
5. After Sadko has sung for the King and Queen of the Ocean, he is promised the hand of Volkhova in marriage. This chorus is sung by all imaginable creatures of the sea and takes place on the ocean floor.

Rimsky-Korsakov, Nicolai. *The Snow Maiden* (*Snegurochka*) (1882)
Librettist: composer, after Ostrovsky
Publishers: Kalmus, Moscow State Music Publishers
354   1. Prologue, "Carnival Chorus"
2. SATB divisi dbl. choir
3. 5.5 minutes
4. Difficult
5. As Spring and Winter depart, a carnival troupe arrives. This joyful double chorus is sung as the people fill the stage.

355   1. Act II, "Palace Chorus"
2. TTBB
3. 5.5 minutes
4. Moderately Difficult
5. A regal chorus, sung in the Tsar's palace.
N.B. A similar but much shorter chorus ends the act.

Rimsky-Korsakov, Nicolai. *Tsar Saltan* (1900)
Librettist: V.I. Byelsky, after Alexander Pushkin
Publisher: Kalmus
356   1. Act I, "Tsarevitch Chorus"
2. SATB divisi
3. 3 minutes
4. Difficult

   5. The people sing a joyful chorus of praise to the
      Tsarevitch. The animated chorus alternates
      between 5/8 and 5/4.

357   1. Act I, "Weeping Chorus"
      2. SATB divisi; several incidental soli
      3. 4.5 minutes
      4. Moderately Difficult
      5. After the Tsarina and the Tsarevitch climb into the
         barrel to be tossed into the sea, the people weep
         and despair.

358   1. Act II, "Welcome Chorus"
      2. SATB divisi dbl. choir; Tsarina (S), Prince Guidon
         (T)
      3. 8 minutes
      4. Difficult
      5. As the Tsarina and the Prince arrive in the city, the
         crowd greets them with a jubilant chorus. The
         Prince accepts the throne of Russia and Act II
         ends with great rejoicing.

Rossini, Gioacchino. *La Cenerentola* (1817)
Librettist: Jacopo Ferretti, after Etienne
Publishers: Broude Bros., Colombo, Fondazione Rossini
   Pesaro (cw), Ricordi, G. Schirmer
359   1. Act I, "O figlie a mabili di Don Magnifico"
      2. SATB
      3. 2 minutes
      4. Easy
      5. The Prince's followers announce a ball and the fact
         that the most beautiful girl in attendance will
         marry him.

360   1. Act I, "Conciosiacosachè trenta botti già gusto'"
      2. SATB
      3. 2 minutes

    4. Easy
    5. In the Prince's drawing room, his courtiers surround
       him and sing in praise of the Baron, who has been
       appointed chief butler. The Baron is quite
       occupied tasting all the available wines.

361   1. Act II, "Della Fortuna instabile"
        2. SAB
        3. 2 minutes
        4. Easy
        5. In the final scene of the opera, all complications are
          resolved. The chorus sings a short passage in
          the elegant royal hall declaring that "virtue reigns!"

Rossini, Gioacchino. *La Donna del Lago* (1819)
Librettist: Andrea Leone Tottola, after Sir Walter Scott
Publishers: Kalmus, Fondazione Rossini Pesaro (cw); G.
  Schirmer
362   1. Act I, Scene 1, "Del dì las messaggiera"
        2. SATB divisi
        3. 3.5 minutes
        4. Medium
        5. On the shores of Lake Katrine in Scotland, choruses
          of shepherds and hunters sing *in alternatim*.
        N.B. The tenor tessitura is high.

363   1. Act I, Scene 1, "Uberto!"
        2. TTBB
        3. 6.5 minutes
        4. Moderately Difficult
        5. While looking for Uberto, the hunters sing a
          rousing, musically varied "search" chorus in 6/8.

364   1. Act I, Scene 3, "Qual rapido torrente"
        2. TTB
        3. 2.5 minutes
        4. Medium

5. In an open field surrounded by mountains, Roderick is welcomed by his clansmen.

365 1. Act I, Scene 3, "Vieni o stella"
2. TTB
3. 2 minutes
4. Moderately Difficult
5. Malcolm and his followers enter stage via this brisk choral march.

366 1. Act II, Scene 2, "Impogna il Re"
2. SATTB
3. 2.5 minutes
4. Moderately Difficult
5. A short chorus hailing the King.

Rossini, Gioacchino. *Elisabetta, Regina d'Inghilterra* (1815)
Librettist: Giovanni Schmidt
Publishers: Broude Bros., Fondazione Rossini Pesaro (cw), Garland, Kalmus, G. Schirmer

367 1. Act I, No. 3, "Vieni, o prode"
2. SATB
3. 2.5 minutes
4. Medium
5. Queen Elizabeth has taken the sons of the Scottish nobility into her service as pages. Here, they are welcomed by the courtiers.

Rossini, Gioacchino. *La Gazza Ladra* (1817)
Librettist: Giovanni Gherardini
Publishers: Fondazione Rossini Pesaro (cw), Kalmus

368 1. Act II, Scene 9, "Tremate, o populi"
2. TTBB
3. 4.5 minutes
4. Moderately Difficult

5. At the town hall, the Tribunal sings imperiously of its many powers, in a chorus full of both grace and strength.

Rossini, Gioacchino. *Guillaume Tell* (1829)
Librettists: Etienne de Jouy and Hippolyte Louis Florent Bis, after Friedrich Schiller
Publishers: Broude Bros., Fondazione Rossini Pesaro (cw), Garland, Kalmus, Ricordi, G. Schirmer

369 1. Act I, No. 1, "Quel jour serein le ciel"
2. SATTB
3. 2 minutes
4. Medium
5. A beautiful morning is dawning on the Lake of Lucerne. The chorus sings of the morning and the upcoming Shepherd Festival.

370 1. Act I, No. 2, "Près des torrens qui grondent"
2. SATTBB
3. 4 minutes
4. Moderately Difficult
5. A joyful choral *galop*, extolling the wonders of love.
N.B. The scene calls for a number of principal voices, all of whose music is doubled in the choral parts.

371 1. Act I, No. 4, "Hyménée, ta journée"
2. SATTB
3. 3.5 minutes
4. Moderately Difficult
5. A chorus extolling the beauty of flowers, bowers, and love.

372 1. Act I, No. 6, "Enfans de la nature"
2. SATTB; Jemmy (S), Hedwiga (S)
3. 4.5 minutes
4. Moderately Difficult

5. A chorus praising Tell's son. The archers march about the stage while singing.

N.B. This and the previous chorus might have been classified in the "medium" difficulty level, if not for the divided tenor part and the high tessitura of the first tenor line.

373   1. Act II, No. 8, "Quelle sauvage harmonie"
2. TTBB/SATTBB dbl. choir; a hunter (B)
3. 3.5 minutes
4. Difficult
5. A chorus of hunters and Switzers.

374   1. Act II, No. 12, "Jurons, jurons par nos dangers"
2. TTBB; Arnold (T), Tell (Bar), Walter (B)
3. 4 minutes
4. Difficult
5. The men of Unterwald, Schwitz and Uri gather. Led by the principals, they swear to be free of Austria.

375   1. Act III, No. 14, "Gloire au pouvoir suprême"
2. SATB divisi; Gessler (B)
3. 8 minutes
4. Difficult
5. Soldiers and peasants sing in praise of Gessler and Austrian rule.

N.B. Several passages of this chorus are scored only for the men or women.

376   1. Act III, No. 15, "Toi que l'oiseau"
2. SATTBB
3. 2 minutes
4. Moderately Difficult
5. A Tyrolean chorus.

N.B. The chorus is reprised later in the same scene.

377   1. Act IV, No. 19, "Amis, secondez vengeance"
       2. TTBB; Arnold (T)
       3. 5.5 minutes
       4. Difficult
       5. Arnold and the men vow to rescue Tell.

Rossini, Gioacchino. *L'Italiana in Algeri* (1813)
Librettist: Angelo Anelli
Publishers: Broude Bros., Fondazione Rossini Pesaro (cw),
    Ricordi, G. Schirmer
378   1. Act I, Scene 1, "Serenate il mesto ciglio"
       2. TTB; Elvira (S), Zulma (M)
       3. 2.5 minutes
       4. Medium
       5. The eunuchs lament while Elvira and Zulma
          discuss matters of love.

379   1. Act I, Scene 4, "Viva, viva il flagel delle donne"
       2. TTB
       3. 2.5 minutes
       4. Moderately Difficult
       5. A chorus of eunuchs sings in honor of Mustafa, the
          "tamer of women."

380   1. Act II, Scene 4, "Pronti abbiamo e ferri e mani"
       2. TTB
       3. 2 minutes
       4. Medium
       5. Italian slaves pledge their willingness to escape
          captivity.

Rossini, Gioacchino. *Mosè in Egitto* (1817)
Librettist: Andrea Leone Tottola
Publishers: Broude Bros., Fondazione Rossini Pesaro (cw),
    Garland, Kalmus, Ricordi, G. Schirmer

381   1. Act I, Scene 1, "Ah! dell' empio al potere feroce"
      2. SATB divisi
      3. 3 minutes
      4. Moderately Difficult
      5. In the camp of the Israelites in Egypt, the people pray for release from their captivity and yearn for their homeland.

382   1. Act III, Scene 1, "O tu che sei"
      2. SATTB
      3. 2.5 minutes
      4. Medium
      5. Egyptians worship a goddess.
      N.B. The tenor tessitura is high; this chorus is reprised after a short interlude sung by Osiride.

Rossini, Gioacchino. *Semiramide* (1823)
Librettist: Gaetano Rossi, after Voltaire
Publishers: Fondazione Rossini Pesaro (cw), Garland, Kalmus, Ricordi, G. Schirmer

383   1. Act I, No. 1b, "Belo si celebri"
      2. SATB divisi
      3. 3.5 minutes
      4. Medium
      5. A joyful, festive chorus to Belus.

384   1. Act I, No. 3, "Di plausi qual clamor"
      2. SATTB
      3. 3 minutes
      4. Medium
      5. A chorus in praise of the Queen, Semiramide.
      N.B. The tenor tessitura is high; the scene also contains numerous other, shorter choral passages.

385   1. Act I, No. 4, "Ergi omai la fronte"
      2. SATTBB
      3. 5 minutes

4. Moderately Difficult
5. A rousing choral march sung by the priests and the people.

386   1. Act II, No. 16, "Ah, la sorte ci tradì"
       2. TTB; Assur (Bar)
       3. 4 minutes
       4. Medium
       5. The people inform Assur of a threat against the throne.

387   1. Act II, No. 17, "Un traditor"
       2. TTBB
       3. 3.5 minutes
       4. Medium
       5. The chorus wishes death to the traitor.

Roussel, Albert. *Padmâvatî* (1923)
Librettist: Louis Laloy
Publisher: Durand
388   1. Act I, Scenes 1 and 2, "Etendez encore"
       2. SATTB; Une femme (S)
       3. 3.5 minutes
       4. Difficult
       5. The people of Chitoor are in the square in front of the palace. They anxiously await the arrival of Alauddin. When he appears, they greet him with a charming chorus sung on neutral vowel syllables.

389   1. Act I, Scene 2, "Dance of the Hindus"
       2. SATB divisi; SA soli
       3. 5.5 minutes
       4. Difficult
       5. Alauddin requests a performance by the Hindu palace dancers, usually only seen by believers. The

extensive, atmospheric dance is accompanied
by a chorus sung on "ah."

390   1. Act II, Scene 1, "Om! Siva"
2. SATB divisi; Padmâvatì (A)
3. 4 minutes
4. Moderately Difficult
5. At dawn, the priests are chanting in the temple.
Padmâvatì has also come to pray for a resolution
of the dangerous situation.

391   1. Act II, Scene 3, "Cérémonie funèbre"
2. SATB divisi; SA soli
3. 14 minutes
4. Difficult
5. An extensive funeral ceremony includes voices
inside and outside of the temple, lamenting the
death of Ratan-Sen and the impending suicide of
Padmâvatì. The chorus is quite complex.

S

Saint-Saëns, Camille. *Samson et Dalila* (1877)
Librettist: Ferdinand Lemaire
Publishers: Broude Bros., Kalmus, G. Schirmer
392   1. Act I, Scene 1, "Dieu! Dieu d'Israël"
2. SATB divisi
3. 8 minutes (5 + 3)
4. Moderately Difficult
5. The opera opens with an extended chorus in two
sections (note timings, above), both expressing the
Jews' despair. The second section is faster and
more dramatic than the first.

393 1. Act I, Scene 6, "Voici le printemps"
2. SSAA
3. 2 minutes
4. Medium
5. Delilah and the Philistine women enter the gates of Dagon's temple holding garlands of flowers.

394 1. Act III, Scene 2, "L'aube qui blanchit"
2. SATB divisi
3. 2.5 minutes
4. Medium
5. In Dagon's temple, the Philistines rejoice by singing about the beauty of the dawn.

395 1. Act III, Scene 3, "Dagon se révèle"
2. SATB divisi; Delilah (M), High Priest (Bar)
3. 4 minutes
4. Difficult
5. While the chorus sings exuberant praises to Dagon, Samson places himself between the two pillars. Delilah and the High Priest lead the incantation.

Schoenberg, Arnold. *Moses und Aron* (1954)
Librettist: composer
Publishers: Broude Bros., B. Schott's Söhne, G. Schirmer
396 1. Act I, Scene 1, "Moses Berufung"
2. SS(boys)ATBB (Voice from the burning bush); SSATBB soli, Moses (speaker)
3. 10 minutes
4. Difficult
5. In the very interesting opening scene of the opera, six solo voices from the orchestra pit portray Moses at prayer, using *sprechstimme*. A semi-chorus, including boy's voices, answers him from the burning bush (also spoken). The choruses then proclaim God's promise that the Israelites are the

chosen people, and Moses is called to lead the people out of bondage with his brother Aron (Aaron) as his spokesman.

N.B. Obviously, this entire work requires vocal and musical skills far beyond most other operas in this volume. The performer is urged to tackle this work with care.

397   1. Act I, Scene 3, "Moses und Aron verkünden"
2. SATB divisi dbl. choir; Mädchen (S)
3. 3 minutes
4. Difficult
5. The priests doubt that a new God will deliver the Israelites from their slavery. A grand chorus, partially spoken and partially sung, proceeds as Moses and Aron are seen approaching from a distance.

398   1. Act I, Scene 4, "Bringt ihr Erhörung"
2. SATB divisi dbl. choir; Moses (speaker), Aron (T), numerous incidental soli
3. 25 minutes
4. Difficult
5. In a mammoth scene that is primarily scored for chorus, Aron performs miracles, and the people in their fervor set off in a great choral march through the desert.

399   1. Interlude, "Wo ist Moses?"
2. SSATBB
3. 2 minutes
4. Difficult
5. In between the two acts of the opera, the chorus sings and speaks a *scherzo* movement in front of the curtain. This hushed search for Moses has a compelling beauty.

400   1. Act II, Scene 2, "Götter, Bilder unsres Auges"
           2. SATB
           3. 4 minutes
           4. Difficult
           5. Approximately half-way through this scene, Aron
              tries to control the crowd by pledging to give the
              gods real form, and the people rejoice.

Smetana, Bedřich. *The Bartered Bride* (*Prodaná Nevěsta*)
   (1866)
Librettist: Karel Sabina
Publishers: Boosey and Hawkes, Broude Bros., Kalmus, G.
Schirmer

401   1. Act I, Scene 1, "Now the time is ripe for mating"
           2. SATB; Marie (S), Jeník (T)
           3. 6 minutes
           4. Medium
           5. It is spring in Bohemia and the villagers are happy
              at the thought of the holiday dancing soon to
              occur. Only Jeník and Marie do not join in the
              fun.
           N.B. The scene may be extended by the inclusion of
           the actual dance following this chorus, which also
           includes a delightful choral passage.

402   1. Act II, Scene 1, "You foam within our glasses"
           2. TTBB; Jeník (T), Kečal (B)
           3. 5 minutes
           4. Difficult
           5. An extremely spirited drinking chorus. Led by the
              two principals, the men sing the praises of beer,
              wealth, women, and fire!

Smetana, Bedřich. *Dalibor* (1870)
Librettist: Joseph Wenzig
Publishers: Broude Bros., Josef Weinberger

403   1. Act II, Scene 3, "Soldiers' Chorus"
     2. TB
     3. 2 minutes
     4. Medium
     5. A soldiers' chorus, where the men exhort one another to drink and love. Includes a generous portion of "fa-la-las."

Smetana, Bedřich. *Libuše* (1881)
Librettist: Josef Wenzig, trans. into Czech by Spindler
Publishers: Broude Bros., Krásné Literatury; OSU

404   1. Act I, "Finale"
     2. SATB divisi; Libuše (S), Radovan (Bar)
     3. 4 minutes
     4. Difficult
     5. In the joyful Finale to Act I, Libuše chooses her childhood sweetheart as her husband-to-be. The ensemble rejoices in a chorus of great rhythmic vitality.

405   1. Act II, Scene 3, "Harvesters' Chorus"
     2. SSAT; T solo
     3. 3 minutes
     4. Difficult
     5. In the countryside, a harvesters' chorus is heard in the distance. The selection is full of interesting effects, including trills and rapidly changing rhythmic patterns.
     N.B. There is a short reprise of the chorus at the end of the scene.

406   1. Act III, Scene 3, "Women's Chorus"
     2. SSAA; Libuše (S)
     3. 4.5 minutes
     4. Difficult
     5. Libuše and the assembled women sing a spirited chorus full of rhythmic and melodic invention.

Smetana, Bedřich. *The Secret* (*Tajemství*) (1878)
Librettist: Eliška Krásnohorská
Publishers: Broude Bros., Státni Literatury; OSU
407   1. Act III, Scene 1, "Hop Harvest Chorus"
      2. SATB
      3. 2 minutes
      4. Medium
      5. Workers celebrate the end of the hop harvest.

Smetana, Bedřich. *The Two Widows* (*Dvě Vdovy*) (1874)
Librettist: Emmanuel Züngel, after Malefille
Publishers: Alkor-Edition Kassel, Broude Bros., Musica Rara
   (cw)
408   1. Act I, No. 1, "Harvest Festival Chorus"
      2. SATB divisi; Karolina (S)
      3. 5.5 minutes
      4. Moderately Difficult
      5. As the opera opens, the villagers sing this highly
         rhythmic chorus inviting Karolina, the lady of the
         manor, to the harvest festival.

Spontini, Gasparo. *La Vestale* (1807)
Librettist: Etienne de Jouy
Publishers: Broude Bros., Garland, Ricordi, G. Schirmer
409   1. Act I, "Di lauri il suol"
      2. SSATB
      3. 6 minutes
      4. Moderately Difficult
      5. A magnificent procession makes its way to the
         temple, as the people sing joyously of the
         victorious General.
      N.B. The large chorus becomes a semi-chorus (SATB
      or TBB) at times during the passage; there is also
      a short reprise of this chorus at the end of the act.
      The opera was originally written in French.

410 1. Act I, Finale, "Della Dea pura seguace"
2. SATBB
3. 2 minutes
4. Medium
5. The chorus very gracefully praises Licinio for his victory.

411 1. Act I, Finale, "La pace questo giorno"
2. SSATTB
3. 4.5 minutes
4. Moderately Difficult
5. Licinio is again praised by the crowd, in a passage of more restrained celebration.

412 1. Act II, Finale, "Da quel fronte"
2. SATB divisi; Sacerdote (B)
3. 4 minutes
4. Difficult
5. The Pontifex Maximus (Sacerdote) leads the chorus in denouncing Giulia, ordering that she be stripped of her veil and ornaments, and then buried alive.

413 1. Act III, "Las Vestale infida mora"
2. ATB/SA dbl. choir
3. 5 minutes
4. Moderately Difficult
5. Giulia is led to the altar by groups of lictors and vestals who sing a somber funeral dirge.

414 1. Act III, "Oh, terrore"
2. SSATTB
3. 2 minutes
4. Moderately Difficult
5. The chorus responds in terror to Giulia's impending descent into the tomb.

415   1. Act III, Finale, "Lieti concenti"
2. SSATTB; Giulia (S), Licinio (T)
3. 6 minutes
4. Difficult
5. The two principals and the assembled crowd rejoice
at Giulia's reprieve from death by singing an
extended dance-like chorus, dedicated to Venus.

Strauss, Johann. *Eine Nacht in Venedig* (1883)
Librettists: F. Zell and Richard Genée
Publishers: Broude Bros., Cranz
416   1. Act I, No. 7, "Zur Serenade"
2. SATTB
3. 4.5 minutes
4. Moderately Difficult
5. An ensemble of serenaders mocks Delacqun with a
lovely choral waltz.

417   1. Act II, No. 12, "Horch von San Marco der Glokken"
2. SATTBB
3. 2 minutes
4. Difficult
5. The chorus announces that at midnight all present
must appear at the Piazza San Marco.
N.B. This scene might be extended to the end of the
act by the addition of the music that follows, including
solo and choral passages.

Strauss, Johann. *Die Fledermaus* (1874)
Librettists: Carl Haffner and Richard Genée, after Henri
Meilhac and Ludovic Halévy
Publishers: Boosey and Hawkes, Broude Bros., Jerona,
Kalmus, G. Schirmer
418   1. Act II, No. 6, "Ein Souper heut' uns winket"
2. SATTB; several short solos
3. 2 minutes

4. Medium
5. A boisterous party is underway at Prince Orlofsky's.

419 1. Act II, No. 11, "Im Feuerstrom der Reben"
2. SATTBB; Adele (S), Orlofsky (M), Eisenstein (T)
3. 3 minutes
4. Moderately Difficult
5. A bubbly chorus in praise of champagne, led by the
principals.
N.B. Although this excerpt is sung primarily by the
principals, the choral singing is too delightful to pass
over. In addition, it has long been considered a
"standard" choral selection from the repertoire. For a
longer scene, the remainder of the Finale might also
be performed.

Strauss, Johann. *Wienerblut* (1899)
Librettists: Viktor Leon and Leo Stein
Publishers: Broude Bros., Cranz

420 1. Act II, No. 6, "Ach wer zählt die vielen Namen"
2. SATTBB
3. 3 minutes
4. Moderately Difficult
5. A ball given by Count Bitowski begins with a joyful
choral *polonaise* sung by the assembled guests.

421 1. Act II, No. 10, "Bei dem Wiener Kongresse"
2. SSA
3. 3.5 minutes
4. Moderately Difficult
5. The women praise both the Vienna Congress and
the Countess.

Strauss, Johann. *Der Zigeunerbaron* (1885)
Librettist: J. Schnitzer, after Jokai
Publishers: Broude Bros., Cranz

422   1. Act III, No. 17, "Hurrah, die Schlacht mitgemacht"
      2. SATTBB
      3. 4 minutes
      4. Moderately Difficult
      5. A grand choral march precedes the Finale of the
         opera, in which all conflicts are resolved.

Strauss, Richard. *Capriccio* (1942)
Librettist: Clemens Krauss
Publishers: Boosey and Hawkes, Broude Bros., G. Schirmer,
   B. Schott's Söhne
423   1. Scene 11, "Das war ein schöner Lärm"
      2. TB divisi; Haushofmeister (B), several incidental
         soli
      3. 7 minutes
      4. Moderately Difficult
      5. After the Countess has left the salon, the servants
         enter to take care of the room, where they
         sing a lengthy passage commenting on the many
         happenings of the day.

Strauss, Richard. *Die Liebe der Danae* (1944)
Librettist: Joseph Gregor
Publishers: Boosey and Hawkes, Broude Bros., G. Schirmer,
   B. Schott's Söhne
424   1. Act I, Scene 1, "Chor der Gläubiger"
      2. TTBB; Pollux (T), 4 Watchmen (B)
      3. 4 minutes
      4. Difficult
      5. In the opening scene of the opera, creditors rush
         the throne room of King Pollux and demand to be
         paid. The King tries to pacify them, but instead
         they plunder what is left in the once glorious
         room.

Strauss, Richard. *Die Frau ohne Schatten* (1919)
Librettist: Hugo von Hofmannsthal
Publisher: Boosey and Hawkes
425   1. Act I, "Chorus of Unborn Children"
        2. SSSAA; Die Frau (S)
        3. 2 minutes
        4. Difficult
        5. In this very interesting and complicated passage, the dyer's wife hears the voices of her unborn children coming from the flames of the fire. She is understandably frightened.

Strauss, Richard. *Friedenstag* (1938)
Librettist: Joseph Gregor
Publishers: Boosey and Hawkes, Broude Bros., G. Schirmer, B. Schott's Söhne
426   1. "Sei uns gegrüßt, leuchtender König"
        2. SATB divisi dbl. choir; Maria (S)
        3. 8.5 minutes
        4. Difficult
        5. An extended and glorious hymn to peace ends this opera.

Stravinsky, Igor. *Oedipus Rex* (1927)
Librettist: Jean Cocteau, after Sophocles; translated into Latin by J. Daniélou
Publishers: Boosey and Hawkes, Broude Bros., G. Schirmer
427   1. Act I, "Kaedit nos pestis"
        2. TTBB
        3. 4 minutes
        4. Difficult
        5. The men of Thebes grieve over the plague which is wiping out the inhabitants of their town.

428   1. Act I, "Solve, solve, solve!"
        2. TTBB; Oedipus (T), Speaker

      3. 4 minutes
      4. Difficult
      5. The chorus pays homage to Minerva, Diana, and
         Phoebus, and welcomes Tiresias.

429   1. Act I, "Gloria"
      2. TTBB
      3. 2 minutes
      4. Moderately Difficult
      5. A glorious chorus extending greetings and accolades
         to Queen Jocasta.

430   1. Act II, "Divum Jocasta"
      2. TTBB; Le Messager (Bar)
      3. 6 minutes
      4. Difficult
      5. The final scene of the opera is lengthy and complex.
         The messenger and the chorus lament Jocasta's
         suicide; when the messenger disappears, the
         chorus sings sympathetically of Oedipus's pathetic
         situation, and then bids him adieu.

Stravinsky, Igor. *The Rake's Progress* (1951)
Librettists: W.H. Auden and Chester Kallman
Publishers: Boosey and Hawkes, Broude Bros., G. Schirmer
431   1. Act I, Scene 2, "With air commanding"
      2. TB/SA/SAATB triple choir
      3. 2 minutes
      4. Medium
      5. A chorus for "whores and roaring boys" set in
         Mother Goose's brothel in London.
      N.B. A rather long orchestral prelude precedes the
      rising of the curtain and this scene.

432   1. Act I, Scene 2, "Soon dawn will glitter"
      2. SATB
      3. 1.5 minutes

4. Easy
5. A second chorus for whores and roaring boys.

433 1. Act I, Scene 2, "The sun is bright"
2. SATB; Nick (Bar)
3. 2 minutes
4. Moderately Difficult
5. The chorus sings joyfully as the scene ends. The excerpt is permeated with the refrain "lanterloo."

434 1. Act III, Scene 1, "Ruin, disaster"
2. SATB; Anne (S)
3. 4 minutes
4. Moderately Difficult
5. As the auction is about to begin, citizens are looking at the items for sale and commenting on the end to which extravagance can lead. Anne enters looking for Tom: the chorus is unable to help her find him.

435 1. Act III, Scene 2, "Leave all love and hope behind"
2. SATB
3. 2 minutes
4. Medium
5. In Bedlam, the chorus sings and dances a minuet, mocking Tom.

Stravinsky, Igor. *Le Rossignol* (*The Nightingale*) (1914)
Librettist: composer and S. Mitousoff, after Hans Christian Andersen
Publisher: Boosey and Hawkes
436 1. Act II, Entr'acte, "Des feux"
2. SAT divisi dbl. choir; SAT soli; La Cuisinière (M)
3. 4 minutes
4. Difficult

5. In this delightful choral entr'acte, the people are in a frenetic search for the nightingale. They request light, and ask the cook to describe the little bird.

Szymanowski, Karol. **King Roger** (*Król Roger*) (1926)
Librettist: Slowa Jaroslawa Iwaszkiewicza
Publisher: Broude Bros., G. Schirmer, Universal Edition
437 1. Act I, "Cathedral Chorus"
2. SATB divisi/SSA divisi dbl. choir; T solo
3. 6 minutes
4. Difficult
5. In a Byzantine cathedral, a service is in progress. The worshippers, in alternation with a boy's chorus, sing a glorious Orthodox psalm setting.
N.B. There are many other fine shorter choral passages throughout the act, scored in a similar manner.

T

Tchaikovsky, Peter Ilitsch. **Eugene Onegin** (*Yevgeny Onyegin*) (1879)
Librettists: composer and K.S. Shilovsky, after Alexander Pushkin
Publishers: Broude Bros., Kalmus, G. Schirmer
438 1. Act I, No. 2, "My tottering legs are aching"
2. SATB divisi; Larina (M), Leader (T)
3. 7 minutes
4. Moderately Difficult
5. A group of reapers is heard first in the distance and then onstage. They present Larina with a decorated sheaf as they sing their folksong; the scene ends with a quick choral dance.

439 1. Act I, No. 11, "Come, sweet maidens, gather here"
2. SSAA
3. 3.5 minutes
4. Medium
5. Maids blissfully sing in the garden as they gather berries.

440 1. Act II, No. 13, "What a surprise!"
2. SATB divisi; Lenski (T), Onegin (Bar), Captain (B)
3. 8 minutes
4. Moderately Difficult
5. A ball is in full swing at Larina's house. Several groups sing solo sections in a grand choral waltz, including the old men, old women, and the young women. The fact that Onegin and Tatiana are dancing causes general gossip.

Tchaikovsky, Peter Ilitsch. *The Maid of Orleans* (*Orleanskaya Dyeva*) (1881)
Librettist: composer, after Zhukovsky and Friedrich Schiller
Publishers: Kalmus, G. Schirmer

441 1. Act I, No. 1, "Chorus of Young Girls"
2. SSAA
3. 2.5 minutes
4. Medium
5. In the small village of Domrémy, young women sing a graceful chorus as they decorate an old oak tree.

442 1. Act I, No. 4, "Peoples' Chorus"
2. SATB divisi
3. 2 minutes
4. Moderately Difficult
5. The people express their anger over and fear of the successful English invasion in this fiery scene. A trio of principals doubles the chorus near the end of the excerpt.

443   1. Act II, No. 19, "Minstrels' Chorus"
          2. unison male voices
          3. 3.5 minutes
          4. Easy
          5. At the royal castle at Chinon, minstrels and
tumblers perform for the King and his mistress.
The lovely tune of this selection could be sung by
the chorus tenor section (as the composer has
indicated), by the entire ensemble, or by a solo
voice.

444   1. Act III, No. 18, "March"
          2. SATB divisi
          3. 11.5 minutes
          4. Difficult
          5. A grand march leads to the coronation of the King.
A number of instrumental interludes separate the
choral passages.

Tchaikovsky, Peter Ilitsch. *Mazeppa* (1884)
Librettists: composer and V.P. Burenin, after Alexander
   Pushkin
Publishers: Kalmus, G. Schirmer

445   1. Act I, No. 4, "Hopak Chorus"
          2. SATB divisi
          3. 3.5 minutes
          4. Medium
          5. The chorus sings a delightful entertainment for
Mazeppa. The singing portion of the scene is
followed by a rousing orchestral *hopak*.

446   1. Act II, No. 13, "Folk Chorus"
          2. SATTB
          3. 4 minutes
          4. Medium
          5. In a field near the scaffold, a crowd sings while
waiting for the executioner's victims to arrive.

N.B. The scene may be lengthened with the addition of the music following for a drunken Cossack and chorus.

Tchaikovsky, Peter Ilitsch. *The Queen of Spades* (*Pikovaya Dama*) (1890)
Librettist: Modest Tchaikovsky, after Alexander Pushkin
Publisher: G. Schirmer
447   1. Act I, No. 1, "Chorus of Children"
      2. children's chorus/SSAA dbl. choir; several incidental spoken lines
      3. 6 minutes
      4. Medium
      5. A delightful chorus set in a summer garden in St. Petersburg. The children frolic while their nurses and governesses talk, seated on benches watching the children play.

448   1. Act I, No. 1, "Chorus of Promenaders"
      2. SATB divisi
      3. 3 minutes
      4. Medium
      5. A breezy chorus of strollers enjoying the warm month of May.

449   1. Act II, No. 11, "Happy and Bent on Enjoyment"
      2. SATB divisi
      3. 2.5 minutes
      4. Medium
      5. A masked ball is in progress in a large reception room. A choir on a platform sings this chorus of welcome.

450   1. Act II, No. 15, "The Empress, the Empress!"
      2. SATB divisi; Master of Ceremonies (T)
      3. 2 minutes
      4. Moderately Difficult

  5. The Master of Ceremonies announces the arrival of
     the Empress and the chorus enthusiastically
     welcomes her.
  N.B. There are several rather short, but delightful
  shepherds' choruses preceding this excerpt, which
  might be combined with it.

451   1. Act III, No. 22, "Pass the wine, let's be merry!"
         2. TTBB
         3. 2 minutes
         4. Medium
         5. In the gambling house, the men sing of wine, youth,
            and merriment as they play cards.

Thomas, Ambroise. *Mignon* (1866)
Librettists: Jules Barbier and Michel Carré, after Johann W.
  von Goethe
Publishers: Broude Bros., Heugel, G. Schirmer
452   1. Act I, No. 1, "Bons bourgeois et notables"
         2. TTBB
         3. 2.5 minutes
         4. Medium
         5. In the courtyard of a German inn, townspeople and
            travelers celebrate together.
         N.B. This chorus is reprised later in the scene.

453   1. Act I, No. 1, "Ah! Chantez"
         2. SATTBB; Philine (S)
         3. 2.5 minutes
         4. Medium
         5. A rousing choral waltz is sung as part of a gypsy
            dance. Philine has a colorful solo passage sung on
            "ah."

454   1. Act I, No. 6, "En route, amis"
         2. SSAA/TTBB/SB triple choir
         3. 3.5 minutes

    4. Moderately Difficult
    5. Choruses of comedians, gypsies, actresses, peasants
       and townspeople sing as they prepare for a
       journey.

455   1. Act II, No. 12b, "La Philine est vraiment divine"
      2. SATTBB
      3. 2 minutes
      4. Medium
      5. At the conclusion of a theatrical performance, a
        short chorus praising Philine is sung by all those
        present.

456   1. Act III, No. 13, "Au souffle léger du vent"
      2. SATTBB, unaccompanied
      3. 4 minutes
      4. Moderately Difficult
      5. A boating chorus, with a harp introduction, is heard
        behind the scenes.
    N.B. A short reprise of the excerpt occurs later in the
    same scene.

Tippett, Michael. *The Ice Break* (1977)
Librettist: composer
Publishers: Broude Bros., G. Schirmer, B. Schott's Söhne
457   1. Act I, Scene 3, "Olá, oló"
      2. SSATB
      3. 1.5 minutes
      4. Difficult
      5. In a fascinating chorus full of shouts, non-pitched
        and pitched, a crowd of fans exuberantly greets a
        Black champion Olympian upon his return.
    N.B. Similar vocal effects are used in several
    succeeding scenes.

458   1. Act II, Scene 4, "Hi there, black man"
      2. SATTB

    3. 2 minutes
    4. Difficult
    5. A black masked chorus rushes onto the stage. They
       mask the Olympian so that he will become one
       with the crowd as they sing this defiant chorus.

459   1. Act II, Scene 6, "Wá wá wá wá wá wá white"
    2. ATBB/SATT divisi dbl. chorus
    3. 2 minutes
    4. Difficult
    5. This highly disturbing chorus pits opposing groups
       of whites and blacks against each other. The
       violence onstage is portrayed vocally by agitated
       chants of repeated figures.

460   1. Act III, Scene 5, "Ready, ready?"
    2. SSATTB divisi
    3. 4 minutes
    4. Difficult
    5. From the score: "Seekers of all kinds, tough and
       tender, past, present and future, are in the
       Paradise Garden: perhaps smoking pipes of peace
       or pot." They sing this highly unusual chorus as
       they get ready for their "trip." Psychedelic colors
       flood the stage.

Tippett, Michael. *King Priam* (1962)
Librettist: composer
Publishers: Broude Bros., G. Schirmer, B. Schott's Söhne
461   1. Act I, "Oh, look there! We could have guessed it"
    2. SATB divisi; several incidental soli
    3. 4 minutes
    4. Difficult
    5. In ancient Troy, guests return from the wedding of
       Andromache and Hector in a joyful mood. Yet,
       they are concerned about the growing hostility
       between Hector and Paris.

Tippett, Michael. *The Midsummer Marriage* (1955)
Librettist: composer
Publishers: Broude Bros., G. Schirmer, B. Schott's Söhne

462 1. Act I, Scene 1, "This way, this way!"
    2. SATB divisi dbl. choir
    3. 3 minutes
    4. Difficult
    5. Friends of Mark and Jenifer arrive for the couple's marriage. They greet the dawning morning in a brilliant double chorus.

463 1. Act II, Scene 1, "Call crying as they're flying"
    2. SATB divisi dbl. choir; Bella (S)
    3. 2.5 minutes
    4. Difficult
    5. An offstage chorus and an onstage semi-chorus celebrate the longest day of midsummer.

464 1. Act III, Scene 1, "For bread is but plain"
    2. SSATB divisi
    3. 2.5 minutes
    4. Difficult
    5. A picnic has just ended and the chorus senses the presence of the King Fisher.

465 1. Act III, Scene 4, "See, see, see, see"
    2. TBB/SSA dbl. choir, later SSATBB
    3. 3.5 minutes
    4. Difficult
    5. The people, beginning in the wings, process onstage carrying a litter containing a cloaked figure.

466 1. Act III, Scene 9, "Even in a summer night"
    2. SATB
    3. 4 minutes
    4. Difficult
    5. The end of the opera alternates sharply between reality and fantasy; the chorus asks, "was it a

vision? was it a dream?" in an extended segment.
Instrumental interludes separate the choral
passages.

V

Vaughan Williams, Ralph. *Hugh the Drover* (1924)
Librettist: Harold Child
Publishers: J. Curwen, Faber; LC
467   1. Act I, "Hurrah!"
       2. SSATTB
       3. 1.5 minutes
       4. Medium
       5. The people sing while preparing John for a fight
          with Hugh. The music is constructed using four
          ostinato motives.

Vaughan Williams, Ralph. *The Pilgrim's Progress* (1951)
Librettist: John Bunyan
Publisher: Oxford
468   1. Act III, Scene 1, "Buy!"
       2. SSATBB
       3. 3 minutes
       4. Moderately Difficult
       5. At Vanity Fair, vendors, dressed in unusual
          costumes of all periods, stand near their booths
          tempting the Pilgrims with all kinds of worldly
          pleasures.

469   1. Act III, Scene 1, "Ah! Hold him!"
       2. SATB divisi
       3. 3.5 minutes
       4. Moderately Difficult

5. The Lord Hate-Good sentences the Pilgrim to prison and death, and the crowd responds with this hate-filled chorus.

470 1. Act IV, Scene 3, "Alleluia"
2. SATB divisi dbl. choir; AT soli
3. 5 minutes
4. Difficult
5. As the Pilgrim's journey is finally over and he is welcomed through the gates of the city, offstage and onstage ensembles sing a glorious chorus of praise.
N.B. The alto and tenor solo parts could be sung by semi-choruses.

Verdi, Giuseppi. *Aïda* (1871)
Librettist: Antonio Ghislanzoni
Publishers: Broude Bros., Dover, International, Kalmus, Ricordi, G. Schirmer

471 1. Act I, Scene 2, "Possente, possente Fthà"
2. SSA/TTBB dbl. choir; High Priestess (S), Ramphis (B)
3. 2.5 minutes
4. Moderately Difficult
5. Inside the Temple of Vulcan at Memphis, the gods are invoked by the High Priestess and the women, and by Ramphis and the men.

472 1. Act I, Scene 2, "Nume, custode e vindice"
2. SSA/TTBB dbl. choir; High Priestess (S), Radamès (T), Ramphis (B)
3. 5.5 minutes
4. Difficult
5. A highly emotional prayer is sung by the two male principals and a chorus of priests outside a temple, and by the High Priestess and the women's ensemble from the interior.

473   1. Act II, Scene 1, "Chi mai, fra gli inni e i plausi"
          2. SSA; Amneris (M)
          3. 3.5 minutes
          4. Medium
          5. Amneris is surrounded by female slaves who are
             dressing her for a celebration feast.
          N.B. The scene may be extended by including the
          following moorish dance, in turn followed by a short
          reprise of this excerpt.

474   1. Act II, Scene 2, "Gloria all' Egitto"
          2. SSTB; TTBB chorus of priests; 3 S soli
          3. 3 minutes
          4. Difficult
          5. A joyous chorus hailing the glories of Eygpt. This
             piece is followed by the well-known "Eygptian
             March."

475   1. Act II, Scene 2, "Vieni, o guerriero vindice"
          2. SSTB/TTBB dbl. choir
          3. 3 minutes
          4. Diffcult
          5. A splendid double chorus of people and priests that
             uses the same musical material as the previous
             excerpt.
          N.B. The Finale of Act II also makes extensive use of
          choral forces.

Verdi, Giuseppe. *Aroldo* (1857)
Librettist: Francesco Maria Piave
Publishers: Broude Bros., Kalmus, Ricordi, G. Schirmer
476   1. Act I, "Coro d'Introduzione"
          2. TTBB, unaccompanied
          3. 2 minutes
          4. Moderately Difficult
          5. This chorus is sung offstage, from the great hall of
             Egberto's castle; the text praises Aroldo.

477   1. Act IV, "Coro d'Introduzione"
      2. SSA/TTBB dbl. choir
      3. 6 minutes
      4. Moderately Difficult
      5. A chorus of shepherds, reaping women and
         huntsmen sings a rollicking pastoral chorus in 6/8
         on the banks of Loch Lomond.

Verdi, Giuseppe. *Un Ballo in Maschera* (1859)
Librettist: Antonio Somma, after Eugène Scribe
Publishers: Boosey and Hawkes, Broude Bros., International,
  Ricordi, G. Schirmer
478   1. Act I, No. 2, "Posa in pace"
      2. TTBB; Samuel (B), Tommaso (B), Loro Aderenti
         (B)
      3. 2 minutes
      4. Moderately Difficult
      5. The courtiers and people sing a peaceful tribute to
         Riccardo.

Verdi, Giuseppe. *La Battaglia di Legnano* (1849)
Librettist: Salvatore Cammarano
Publishers: Broude Bros., Kalmus, Ricordi, G. Schirmer
479   1. Act I, "Coro di Donzelle"
      2. SSA
      3. 3.5 minutes
      4. Medium
      5. In a shady place, maidens gently sing with Lida, the
         wife of the Duke of Milan; this chorus contrasts
         with Lida's following aria, which details the
         horrors of war.

480   1. Act II, "Coro d'Introduzione"
      2. TTBB
      3. 3 minutes
      4. Moderately Difficult

5. In Como, a group of Dukes and magistrates sings as
they assemble to receive a deputation from the
League.

Verdi, Giuseppe. *Don Carlo*
Librettist: Joseph Méryand Camille du Locle, after Friedrich
   Schiller
Publishers: Broude Bros., Kalmus, Ricordi, G. Schirmer
481   1. Act I, Part 1, "Carlo il sommo Imperature"
            2. TTBB; Un Frate (B)
            3. 4.5 minutes
            4. Moderately Difficult
            5. A friar kneels before a tomb in prayer, while a
               chorus of friars is heard offstage.

482   1. Act I, Part 2, "Sotto ai folti"
            2. SSA; Tebaldo (S), Eboli (M)
            3. 4.5 minutes
            4. Medium
            5. In the garden of the monastery of St. Just, the
               Princess of Eboli, Tebaldo and other ladies-in-
               waiting sit on the grassy mounds around the
               fountain and sing of the beauty surrounding them.

483   1. Act II, Part 2, "Spuntato ecco il dí d'esultanza"
            2. SATB divisi/unison men's chorus
            3. 9 minutes
            4. Difficult
            5. A splendid processional passes in front of a tomb.
               The monks also cross the stage (singing in unison),
               leading the condemned man to the stake.
            N.B. There is a lengthy instrumental interlude in the
            middle of this excerpt.

Verdi, Giuseppe. *I Due Foscari* (1844)
Librettist: Francesco Maria Piave, after Lord Byron
Publishers: Broude Bros., Kalmus, Ricordi, G. Schirmer

484   1. Act I, "Silenzio, mistero"
      2. TTBB; Barbarigo (T), Loredano (B)
      3. 6 minutes
      4. Medium
      5. The Council of Trent is gathered in a room in the
         Doge's Palace. In a chorus full of rapid dynamic
         shifts, the men sing importantly of the weight and
         finality of their decisions.

485   1. Act I, "Tacque il reo!"
      2. TTBB
      3. 2.5 minutes
      4. Medium
      5. A chorus of Senators.
      N.B. There are two principal roles, for Barbarigo (T)
      and Loredano (B), but their parts are always doubled
      in the choral lines.

486   1. 1. Act II, "Che più si tarda?"
      2. TTBB
      3. 4 minutes
      4. Medium
      5. The Council waits for Jacopo in the great hall. They
         discuss the unchanging Venetian judicial system.

487   1. Act III, "Alla gioia, alle corse, alle gare"
      2. SATB divisi; Barbarigo (T), Loredano (B)
      3. 5 minutes
      4. Moderately Difficult
      5. The plaza of San Marco is brimming with masked
         partygoers enjoying the carnival. This brilliant,
         festive chorus leads into a lilting *barcarolle*, sung
         by the gondoliers.

Verdi, Giuseppe. *Ernani* (1844)
Librettist: Francesco Maria Piave, after Victor Hugo
Publishers: Broude Bros., Kalmus, Ricordi

488   1. Act I, "Evviva! beviam!"
2. TTBB
3. 4 minutes
4. Moderately Difficult
5. A rousing chorus of rebel mountaineers.

489   1. Act II, "Esultiamo!"
2. SATTBB
3. 4 minutes
4. Medium
5. In the grand hall of Silva's castle, a crowd of women, maids, pages and cavaliers sings of the beauty and virtue of the bride-to-be.

490   1. Act II, Finale, "In arcione, in arcion, cavalieri"
2. TTBB; Ernani (T), Silva (B)
3. 2.5 minutes
4. Difficult
5. A lively choral call to arms, led by the two principals: "To horse! to horse, cavaliers!"

491   1. Act III, "Si ridesti il Leon di Castiglia"
2. TBB
3. 3 minutes
4. Moderately Difficult
5. An excited chorus of conspirators, led by Ernani, Silva and Jago (whose lines are all doubled in the choral parts).

492   1. Act IV, "Oh come felici"
2. SATB divisi
3. 3 minutes
4. Moderately Difficult
5. On the terrace of Ernani's castle, a masked ball begins with this rousing chorus.

Verdi, Giuseppe. *Falstaff* (1893)
Librettist: Arrigo Boito, after William Shakespeare
Publishers: Broude Bros., Dover, Kalmus, International,
Ricordi, G. Schirmer
493   1. Act III, Scene 2, "Ruzzola, ruzzola!"
      2. TTB/SSSAA dbl. choir; Alice (S), Meg (M), Quickly
         (A), Falstaff (Bar)
      3. 2 minutes
      4. Moderately Difficult
      5. Choruses of spirits and imps, as well as humans,
         taunt and mystify Falstaff.

Verdi, Giuseppe. *La Forza del Destino* (1862)
Librettist: Francesco Maria Piave, after the Duke of Rivas
Publishers: Boosey and Hawkes, Broude Bros., Dover,
Kalmus, Ricordi, G. Schirmer
494   1. Act III, Scene 6, "Compagni, sostiamo"
      2. TTBB
      3. 3 minutes
      4. Medium
      5. A patrol enters the grounds of a military camp near
         Velletri to inspect them.

495   1. Act III, Scene 10, "Lorchè pifferi e tamburi"
      2. SATTBB; Preziosilla (M)
      3. 4 minutes
      4. Moderately Difficult
      5. It is sunrise in the military camp: the soliders go
         about their duties, vivandieres sell their wares, and
         Preziosilla (a gypsy) tells fortunes.
      N.B. Preziosilla's final passage is quite florid.

496   1. Act III, Scene 14, "Nella guerra è la follia"
      2. SATB divisi; Preziosilla (M)
      3. 2.5 minutes
      4. Medium

      5. The vivandieres and the young recruits sing and
         dance a very lively *tarantella*.
      N.B. Much of Preziosilla's music is doubled in the
      chorus. Scenes 12 and 13 which precede this chorus
      combine to form an interesting dialogue between
      Preziosilla and the choruses of recruits and
      vivandieres.

497   1. Act III, Scene 14, "Rataplan"
        2. SATB divisi; Preziosilla (M)
        3. 3 minutes
        4. Difficult
        5. Preziosilla leads a lively march to end the act.
        N.B. Much of this excerpt is unaccompanied.

Verdi, Giuseppe. *Un Giorno di Regno* (1840)
Librettist: Felice Romani
Publisher: Kalmus
498   1. Act I, Scene 1, "Mai no rise"
        2. SATB divisi
        3. 3.5 minutes
        4. Medium
        5. In the hall of the castle, the baron's servants are
          busily making preparations for the upcoming
          double wedding.

499   1. Act I, Scene 2, "Sì festevole mattina"
        2. SSAA
        3. 2.5 minutes
        4. Easy
        5. In the garden of the castle, young peasant girls
          envelop Giulietta with gifts of fruit and flowers.

500   1. Act II, Scene 1, "Ma le nozze non si fanno?"
        2. TTB
        3. 4 minutes
        4. Medium

5. Because of the indecision of the aristocrats, the male servants are unsure whether or not the wedding is going to take place.

N.B. The tenor tessitura is high.

Verdi, Giuseppe. *Giovanna d'Arco* (1845)
Librettist: Temistocle Solera, after Friedrich Schiller
Publishers: Broude Bros., Kalmus, Ricordi, G. Schirmer

501   1. Prologue, "Qual v'ha speme?"
2. SATB divisi/TTBB dbl. choir
3. 3.5 minutes
4. Medium
5. In Dom-Rémy, the villagers and some of the King's officers await word of his impending surrender to the English troops.

502   1. Prologue, "Allor che i flebili"
2. SATB divisi
3. 3.5 minutes
4. Medium
5. The villagers tell the King that the place in the forest at which he has decided to abdicate is a place of horror and death. This colorful chorus describes the haunted location.

N.B. The tenor tessitura is high.

503   1. Prologue, "Tu sei bella!"
2. SATB divisi/A (angels) dbl. choir
3. 4 minutes
4. Medium
5. In this highly unique chorus, demons tempt Giovanna (Joan of Arc) in her sleep with sensual dreams. In sharp conrast, angels provide her a vision of putting on her sword and helmet and rescuing France.

504   1. Act I, "Ai laril alla patria"
2. TTBB; Talbot (B)
3. 4 minutes
4. Moderately Difficult
5. Near Rheims, Talbot, the English commander,
tries to encourage his soldiers as they sense
looming defeat.

Verdi, Giuseppe. *I Lombardi* (1843)
Librettist: Temistocle Solera
Publishers: Broude Bros., Kalmus, Ricordi, G. Schirmer
505   1. Act I, Scene 1, "O nobile esempio!"
2. TTB/S dbl. choir, later SATB divisi
3. 6 minutes
4. Moderately Difficult
5. A crowd in a piazza in Milan hears the sounds of
rejoicing from inside the cathedral, which include
both a unison women's chorus and a band, and
they comment on this strange circumstance.

506   1. Act II, Scene 1, "È dunque vero?"
2. TTBB; Acciano (B)
3. 4 minutes
4. Moderately Difficult
5. In Acciano's palace in Antioch, the enthroned
Acciano receives a group of Muslim ambassadors.
The visitors invoke Allah's wrath on the invading
army of crusaders.

507   1. Act II, Scene 3, "La bella straniera"
2. SSAA
3. 3 minutes
4. Medium
5. The assembled harem in Acciano's palace taunts
Giselda.

508   1. Act III, Scene 1, "Gerusalem!"
2. SATB divisi
3. 7 minutes
4. Moderately Difficult
5. In the valley of Jehoshaphat, with the Mount of Olives and Jerusalem in sight, a group of pilgrims sings a processional chorus of deep devotion.

509   1. Act IV, Scene 2, "O Signore, dal tetto natio"
2. SATTBB
3. 3.5 minutes
4. Medium
5. The crusaders sing a very effective chorus of longing, similar in style to "Va, pensiero" from Verdi's *Nabucco* (see below).

Verdi, Giuseppe. *Luisa Miller* (1849)
Librettist: Salvatore Cammarano, after Friedrich Schiller
Publishers: Broude Bros., Kalmus, Ricordi, G. Schirmer

510   1. Act I, Introduzione, "Ti desta, Luisa"
2. SATTBB; Laura (A)
3. 4 minutes
4. Medium
5. A peasant chorus set in a village in the Tyrol. The excerpt is sung entirely *mezza voce*.
N.B. Laura sings with the choral altos.

511   1. Act I, "Sciogliete i levrieri"
2. SATTBB dbl. choir; Luisa (S), Miller (Bar)
3. 2.5 minutes
4. Difficult
5. A double chorus of hunters; the two groups are placed on either side of the stage.

Verdi, Giuseppe. *Macbeth* (1847)
Librettist: Francesco Maria Piave, after William Shakespeare
Publisher: Broude Bros., Kalmus, Ricordi, G. Schirmer

512   1. Act I, Scene 1, "Che faceste? Dite su!"
        2. SSSA
        3. 5 minutes
        4. Moderately Difficult
        5. A chorus of witches.

513   1. Act I, Scene 1, "S'allontanarono!"
        2. SSA
        3. 3 minutes
        4. Medium
        5. Another witches chorus.

514   1. Act II, Scene 2, "Chi v'impose unirvi a noi?"
        2. TTBB
        3. 3.5 minutes
        4. Medium
        5. In a park near Macbeth's castle, a band of assassins
           is waiting for Banquo.

515   1. Act III, "Tre volta miagola la gatta in fregola"
        2. SSSA
        3. 5.5 minutes
        4. Moderately Difficult
        5. A third witches chorus, sung around a cauldron in a
           dark cave.

516   1. Act III, "Ondine e solfidi"
        2. SSA
        3. 3.5 minutes
        4. Easy
        5. After Macbeth loses consciousness, the witches
           dance and sing around him before disappearing.

517   1. Act IV, Scene 1, "Patria oppressa!"
        2. SATB divisi
        3. 4 minutes
        4. Medium
        5. A rather reserved chorus of Scottish exiles.

518 1. Act IV, Scene 4, "Macbeth, Macbeth ov'è?"
2. TTB/TTB/SSA triple choir; Macduff (T), Malcolm (T)
3. 4 minutes
4. Difficult
5. A chorus of joy and triumph at the defeat of the tyrant. Crowds of bards, soldiers, and women all join their voices together.

Verdi, Giuseppe. *Nabucco* (1842)
Librettist: Temistocle Solera
Publishers: Broude Bros., Kalmus, Ricordi, G. Schirmer
519 1. Act I, "Gli arredi festivi"
2. SATB divisi; Leviti (Bar)
3. 6 minutes
4. Difficult
5. The priest and the people of Jerusalem sing a chorus lamenting defeat by Nabucodnosor (Nabucco), the King of Babylon.
N.B. The middle section of the chorus is scored for three-part women's chorus.

520 1. Act III, "È l'Assiria una regina"
2. SATB divisi
3. 3.5 minutes
4. Moderately Difficult
5. The people and the high priests demand the death of the Jews held captive.

521 1. Act III, "Va, pensiero"
2. SSATTB
3. 4 minutes
4. Medium
5. This well-known excerpt is one of the composer's most famous patriotic choruses. The captive Hebrew slaves sing of their lost fatherland.

Verdi, Giuseppe. *Otello* (1887)
Librettist: Arrigo Boito
Publishers: Broude Bros., Dover, International, Kalmus,
    Ricordi, G. Schirmer

522   1. Act I, Scene 1, "Esultate! L'orgoglio mulsamano"
        2. SATB divisi; Otello (T)
        3. 3 minutes
        4. Difficult
        5. A victory chorus following a stormy sea voyage.
           Otello greets the people and they respond with
           enthusiasm.

523   1. Act I, Scene 1, "Fuoco di gioia!"
        2. SATB divisi
        3. 4.5 minutes
        4. Difficult
        5. A chorus sung while a huge fire is lit on the
           shore, illuminating the harbor. The music reflects
           the full flame of the fire as well as its flickering
           and dying away.
        N.B. Verdi specifies several different solo groups
        within the larger chorus.

524   1. Act I, "Inaffia l'ugola!"
        2. SATB divisi; Cassio (T), Roderigo (T), Iago (Bar)
        3. 5 minutes
        4. Difficult
        5. The principals lead a rollicking and extended
           drinking song.
        N.B. The solo sections in this passage are extensive.

525   1. Act II, Scene 3, "Dove guardi splendono raggi"
        2. SSSTTBB, unison children's chorus; Desdemona
           (S), Otello (T), Iago (Bar)
        3. 5 minutes
        4. Difficult

5. Women, children, and soldiers surround Desdemona in the garden, singing and strewing flowers. Iago lurks in the background.

Verdi, Giuseppe. *Rigoletto* (1851)
Librettist: Francesco Maria Piave, after Victor Hugo
Publishers: Broude Bros., Dover, International, Kalmus, Ricordi, G. Schirmer
526   1. Act I, No. 10, "Zitti, zitti moviamo a vendetta"
       2. TTBB; Borsa (T), Marcello (Bar), Ceprano (B)
       3. 2 minutes
       4. Moderately Difficult
       5. Nobles, courtiers, and the three principals tiptoe about in the darkness, intent on seeking revenge on Rigoletto. The chorus is sung primarily *sotto voce* and at a *pianissimo* dynamic.
       N.B. In this and the following chorus, the principals are usually doubled in the choral parts.

527   1. Act II, No. 11, "Scorrendo uniti remota via"
       2. TTBB; Duke (T), Borsa (T), Marcello (Bar), Ceprano (B)
       3. 3 minutes
       4. Medium
       5. The three men and the gathered courtiers tell the Duke that they have kidnapped Rigoletto's *inamorata*.

Verdi, Giuseppe. *Simon Boccanegra* (1857)
Librettist: Francesca Maria Piave, after Gutiérrez
Publishers: Associated Music Publishers, Broude Bros., Kalmus, Ricordi, G. Schirmer
528   1. Act II, "Battle Chorus"
       2. SATB divisi; Amelia (S), Gabriele (T), Doge (Bar)
       3. 2.5 minutes
       4. Moderately Difficult

     5. A battle chorus is heard outside. Boccanegra (the
       Doge) orders Gabriele to join his comrades.
       Gabriele swears loyalty to the Doge and promises
       to put an end to the fighting.

Verdi, Giuseppe. *La Traviata* (1853)
Librettist: Francesco Maria Piave
Publishers: Boosey and Hawkes, Broude Bros., Dover,
   International, Kalmus, Ricordi, G. Schirmer
529   1. Act I, No. 3, "Libiamo ne' lieti calici"
       2. SATB divisi; Violetta (S), Alfredo (T)
       3. 5 minutes
       4. Moderately Difficult
       5. Alfredo leads this famous drinking song at Violetta's
         lavish party. The two principals engage in some
         light dialogue and lead the chorus to an
         exuberant climax.
       N.B. Other principal characters double the choral
       parts throughout.

530   1. Act I, No. 5, "Si ridesta in ciel l'aurora"
       2. SATB divisi
       3. 4 minutes
       4. Difficult
       5. A rousing *allegro vivo* chorus sung after the guests
         return from the ballroom, inspired by the dancing.
         After saying their goodbyes, the guests leave.
       N.B. The excerpt calls for several principals, but their
       roles are all doubled in the chorus.

531   1. Act II, No. 12, "Noi siamo zingarelle"
       2. SAA; Flora (M), Marquis (B), Doctor (B)
       3. 3.5 minutes
       4. Moderately Difficult
       5. At Flora's, the women (dressed as gypsies) "read"
         the hands of both Flora and the Marquis, revealing
         his wandering eye. An argument ensues, but the

Doctor and the gypsies urge a new beginning to
the relationship. The gypsies play tambourines
throughout the scene.

532 1. Act II, No. 13, "Di Madride noi siam mattadori"
2. SATB divisi; Flora (M), Marquis (B), Doctor (B)
3. 4.5 minutes
4. Moderately Difficult
5. At Flora's, men dressed as matadors and picadors
tell the tale of a young matador. Led by Gaston,
the scene climaxes as the crowd begins to gamble.
N.B. A good portion of this chorus is scored for TTB.

533 1. Act III, No. 17, "Largo al quadrupede"
2. SSTTB
3. 1.5 minutes
4. Moderately Difficult
5. A lively offstage carnival chorus.

Verdi, Giuseppe. *Il Trovatore* (1853)
Librettist: Salvatore Cammarano, after Gutiérrez
Publishers: Boosey and Hawkes, Broude Bros., International,
Kalmus, Ricordi, G. Schirmer

534 1. Act II, No. 7, "Vedi! le fosche notturne spoglie"
2. SATB
3. 4 minutes
4. Medium
5. This is the famous "Anvil Chorus." The gypsies are
working at their forges and clanking their
hammers in rhythm to the music.
N.B. There is a short reprise of this chorus later in the
same scene.

535 1. Act III, No. 16, "Or co'dadi, ma fra poco"
2. TTBB; Ferrando (B)
3. 6 minutes
4. Moderately Difficult

5. At the camp of the Count di Luna, soldiers and
   Ferrando sing a rousing military chorus.
N.B. Verdi specifies several passages for specific
groups of soldiers; these could be sung by semi-
choruses or the excerpt may be sung *tutti* throughout.

Verdi, Giuseppe. *I Vespri Siciliani* (1855)
Librettist: Eugène Scribe
Publishers: Broude Bros., Kalmus, Ricordi, G. Schirmer
536   1. Act V, "Si celebri al fine tracanti"
         2. TTBB/SSAA dbl. choir
         3. 4 minutes
         4. Difficult
         5. Separate ensembles of cavaliers and young women
            sing a chorus in the gardens of Monfort's palace
            prior to an upcoming wedding.

W

Wagner, Richard. *Der Fliegende Holländer* (1843)
Librettist: composer, after Heinrich Heine
Publishers: Broude Bros., Dover, Eulenberg, Jerona, G.
   Schirmer, B. Schott's Söhne
537   1. Act II, No. 6, "Summ' und brumm'" ("Spinning
            Chorus")
         2. SSAA; Senta (S), Mary (A)
         3. 10 minutes
         4. Moderately Difficult
         5. In Daland's house, Mary and the young girls are
            sitting by the fireplace spinning. The girls tease
            Senta because she is staring at a picture of the
            Flying Dutchman.

N.B. There are several passages within this excerpt which could be eliminated to make a shorter chorus.

538   1. Act II, No. 7, "Das Schiffsvolk kommt"
2. SSAA; Mary (A)
3. 2 minutes
4. Moderately Difficult
5. Mary and the maidens hurry out to meet the sailors.

539   1. Act III, No. 13, "Steuermann! Lass die Wacht!"
2. TTBB/SSAA dbl. choir; Sterrsman (T)
3. 10.5 minutes
4. Difficult
5. In the bay, the two ships, Daland's and the Dutchman's, are next to each other. The Norwegian sailors and the maidens are joyously calling to the Dutch ship, but no response is heard.

540   1. Act III, No. 13, "Johohe!"
2. TTBB dbl. choir
3. 4 minutes
4. Difficult
5. The crew of the Dutchman responds to the taunts of the Norwegians in the previous chorus. A storm rages around *only* the Norwegian vessel and her sailors leave the deck overcome with terror.

Wagner, Richard. *Götterdämmerung* (1876)
Librettist: composer
Publishers: Broude Bros., Dover, Eulenberg, Jerona, Kalmus, G. Schirmer, B. Schott's Söhne

541   1. Act II, Scene 3, "Was tos't das Horn?"
2. TTTBBB
3. 2 minutes
4. Difficult
5. A choral call to arms.

N.B. This excerpt does not have a clear ending and one will need to be fashioned by the conductor. The opening of the chorus calls for several solo voices.

542   1. Act II, Scene 3, "Gross Glück und Heil"
       2. TTTBBB
       3. 1.5 minutes
       4. Moderately Difficult
       5. A hearty chorus of vassals sings of good fortune, health, and Hagen, "the grim one."
       N.B. The choral tessituras here are high. Again, the conductor will need to find a clear ending for the excerpt.

Wagner, Richard. *Lohengrin* (1850)
Librettist: composer
Publishers: Broude Bros., Da Capo Press, Dover, International, Jerona, Kalmus, Ricordi, G. Schirmer, B. Schott's Söhne

543   1. Act I, Scenes 2-3, "Seht! Welch ein seltsam Wunder!"
       2. TTBB, TTBB, then SATB
       3. 4 minutes
       4. Difficult
       5. A men's chorus is the first to see the swan drawing a boat by a golden chain and carrying Lohengrin. The second male chorus is next to view the arrival. As the boat reaches the shore, the mixed chorus greets the knight.

544   1. Act II, Scene 3, "In Früh'n versammelt"
       2. TTBB divisi dbl. choir
       3. 3 minutes
       4. Difficult
       5. The day is dawning and trumpet fanfares have sounded. The nobles and fortress inhabitants sing

of the new, fair morning and of the promise it brings.

545 1. Act II, Scene 3, "Zum Streite"
    2. TTBB dbl. choir
    3. 3.5 minutes
    4. Difficult
    5. A brilliant chorus leading to battle.

546 1. Act II, Scene 4, "Gesegnet soll sie schreiten"
    2. TTBB dbl. choir, then SSA added
    3. 3.5 minutes
    4. Difficult
    5. A glorious polychoral paean to Elsa.

547 1. Act III, Scene 1, "Treulich geführt ziehet"
    2. SSATTB/SSAA dbl. choir
    3. 5.5 minutes
    4. Medium
    5. The famous "Bridal Chorus" is sung as Elsa and Lohengrin are wed. A short choral interlude is sung by eight women after the initial procession.

Wagner, Richard. *Die Meistersinger von Nürnberg* (1868)
Librettist: composer
Publishers: Broude Bros., Dover, International, Jerona, Kalmus, Ricordi, G. Schirmer, B. Schott's Söhne

548 1. Act I, Scene 1, "Da zu dir der Heiland kam"
    2. SATB
    3. 2 minutes
    4. Medium
    5. The congregation in St. Katherine's sings a hymn to open the opera. Walther and Eva attempt to make eye contact during the interludes in the hymn.

549 1. Act III, Scene 5, "Sankt Krispin, lobet ihn!"
    2. TTBB/TTBB/TTBB/ATB divisi

3. 9 minutes
4. Difficult
5. In rapid succession, the cobblers, the tailors and the
   bakers each sing a chorus as part of the jubilant
   festival. At the end, the apprentices speed to the
   waterfront to greet a boatload of young peasant
   girls.

550   1. Act III, Scene 5, "Silentium! Silentium!"
       2. SATB divisi
       3. 6 minutes
       4. Difficult
       5. As the masters arrive at the festival, the assembled
          crowd sings a noble chorus set to the words of
          Hans Sachs.

Wagner, Richard. *Parsifal* (1882)
Librettist: composer
Publishers: Broude Bros., Dover, International, Kalmus,
    Ricordi, G. Schirmer, B. Schott's Söhne
551   1. Act I, "Zum letzten Liebesmahle"
       2. TB/ATTT/SSSA
       3. 5 minutes
       4. Difficult
       5. In turn, the knights of the grail, the youths, and the
          boys sing to the Lord from various locations in the
          pillared hall where a feast is held.

552   1. Act I, "Wein und Brod"
       2. SSATTTBB
       3. 6 minutes
       4. Difficult
       5. As the sacrament is shared, the boys, youths, and
          knights unite in song.
       N.B. The excerpt includes several sustained passages
       for the boys (S) and the youths (A).

553   1. Act II, "Hier! Hier war das Tosen!"
      2. SSSA dbl. choir; 6 S soli
      3. 4 minutes
      4. Difficult
      5. The flower maidens are very upset about the fate of
         their lovers, the knights. They come to the stage
         from all sides of the theatre with anguished cries.

554   1. Act II, "Komm'! Komm'! Holder Knabe!"
      2. SSA dbl. choir; 6 S soli
      3. 2.5 minutes
      4. Difficult
      5. Maidens are festooned with flowers as they
         surround Parsifal and sing this sensuous chorus.

Wagner, Richard. *Rienzi* (1842)
Librettist: composer, after Lytton
Publishers: Broude Bros., Eulenberg, Jerona, Kalmus, G.
   Schirmer, B. Schott's Söhne
555   1. Act I, Finale, "Gegrüßt, gegrüßt sei hoher Tag!"
      2. SSTBB dbl. choir
      3. 4 minutes
      4. Moderately Difficult
      5. A chorus built in two sections: the first is a rousing
         greeting of the Roman morning, and the second
         (preceded by an organ interlude), a prayerful
         double chorus in thanks for liberty.

556   1. Act II, Finale, "Erschallet, Feierklänge"
      2. SSTTB
      3. 3.5 minutes
      4. Medium
      5. A crowd of nobles and Roman citizens sings in
         celebration of peace and freedom. A lengthy
         orchestral introduction precedes the chorus.

557   1. Act III, Finale, "Heil! Heil!"
        2. SSSTTB
        3. 2 minutes
        4. Moderately Difficult
        5. A rousing victory chorus, sung by Roman warriors,
           priests, and monks.

558   1. Act III, Finale, "Auf! Auf!"
        2. SSSTTB
        3. 2.5 minutes
        4. Moderately Difficult
        5. The messenger of peace arrives, Rienzi is crowned
           with a laurel wreath, and the troops march past
           carrying their war trophies.

559   1. Act V, Finale, "Herbei! Herbei!"
        2. SSTTBB
        3. 2.5 minutes
        4. Difficult
        5. A fiery chorus is sung by crowds of people who
           doom Rienzi to death.

Wagner, Richard. *Tannhäuser* (1845)
Librettist: composer
Publishers: Broude Bros., Da Capo Press, Dover, Eulenberg,
    International, Kalmus, Edition Peters, Ricordi, G. Schirmer,
    B. Schott's Söhne
560   1. Act I, Scene 3, "Zu dir wallich" ("Pilgrims' Chorus")
        2. TTBB; Shepherd (S), Tannhäuser (T)
        3. 4.5 minutes
        4. Moderately Difficult
        5. The well-known Pilgrims chorus begins in the
           distance and gradually becomes louder as the elder
           pilgrims get closer. As they cross the stage, they
           bow in front of the crucifix.
        N.B. Much of the choral singing is unaccompanied.

561 1. Act II, Scene 4, "Freudig begrüssen wir die edle Halle"
2. TTTBBB/SSAA dbl. choir
3. 5 minutes
4. Moderately Difficult
5. Knights, nobles and ladies arrive for the Tournament of Song in this grand choral march.

562 1. Act III, Scene 1, "Beglückt darf nun dich"
2. TTBB; Elisabeth (S), Wolfram (Bar)
3. 6 minutes
4. Moderately Difficult
5. The return of the pilgrims, using the same melody as in the overture and in the first act (see above).
N.B. This setting is more fully orchestrated than the excerpt annotated before it. The chorus returns again in the finale.

Wallace, Vincent. *Maritana* (1845)
Librettist: Edward Fitzhall
Publisher: Boosey and Hawkes

563 1. Act I, Scene 1, "Sing, pretty maiden, sing"
2. SATTBB
3. 4.5 minutes
4. Medium
5. On a square in Madrid, Maritana, a street singer, is surrounded by a group of admirers who sings this delightful chorus in praise of her vocal abilities.
N.B. At times, the tenor tessitura is high.

564 1. Act I, Scene 1, "Angelus"
2. SATTB
3. 3 minutes
4. Easy
5. At the ringing of the church bells, the people kneel and sing this lyrical prayer.

565   1. Act II, Scene 2, "Oh, what pleasure"
       2. SATB divisi
       3. 3 minutes
       4. Medium
       5. At the palace of the Marquis Montefiori, the guests
          sing this choral *polacca*.

Walton, William. *Troilus and Cressida* (1954)
Librettist: Christopher Hassall
Publishers: Oxford, G. Schirmer
566   1. Act I, "Virgin of Troas"
       2. SATB divisi dbl. choir; Calkas (B)
       3. 7.5 minutes
       4. Difficult
       5. Choruses of worshippers, priests, and the crowd
          outside the Temple of Pallas are all represented in
          this opening scene to the opera. As the chorus
          unfolds, the prayers become increasingly
          desperate. Calkas, the high priest, attempts to
          calm the people.

Weber, Carl Maria von. *Euryanthe* (1823)
Librettist: Helmine von Chezy
Publisher: Steiner
567   1. Act I, No. 1, "Dem Frieden Heil"
       2. SA/TTBB dbl. choir, then SATB
       3. 4 minutes
       4. Medium
       5. Set in the royal court of Louis VI, the women sing a
          gentle passage which is answered by a chorus of
          knights.
       N.B. The first tenor tessitura is rather high.

568   1. Act I, No. 9, "Jubeltöne Heldensöhne"
       2. SATB/BB dbl. choir
       3. 2.5 minutes

4. Medium
5. A group of peasants welcomes Lysiart, answered by a company of knights.

569 1. Act II, No. 14, "Du gleissend Bild du bist enthüllt!"
2. TTBB; Euryanthe (S)
3. 3.5 minutes
4. Difficult
5. As Adolar leads Euryanthe from the court, the men's chorus dramatically denounces her.

570 1. Act III, No. 18, "Die Thale dampfen die Höhen glühn!"
2. TTBB
3. 2 minutes
4. Moderately Difficult
5. A jubilant hunters' chorus, replete with horns and trombones.

571 1. Act III, No. 21, "Der May bringt frische Rosen dar"
2. SATB; Bertha (S)
3. 3.5 minutes
4. Medium
5. In Nevers, Bertha and the chorus sing a delightfully lilting 6/8 passage extolling the beauty of May.

Weber, Carl Maria von. *Der Freischütz* (1821)
Librettist: Johann Friedrich Kind
Publishers: Boosey and Hawkes, Broude Bros., Dover, Eulenberg, Jerona, Kalmus, G. Schirmer
572 1. Act I, No. 1, "Victoria! Victoria!"
2. SATB
3. 1.5 minutes
4. Medium
5. Kilian, a peasant, has just defeated Max at the target range. The chorus acclaims the victor.

573 1. Act I, No. 2, "Jetzt auf!"
     2. TTB/SATB dbl. choir; Cuno (B)
     3. 3 minutes
     4. Difficult
     5. Companies of huntsmen and villagers bring the
        archery competition to an end.

574 1. Act III, No. 14, "Wir winden dir den Jungfernkranz"
     2. SA; 4 M soli
     3. 2 minutes
     4. Easy
     5. Bridesmaids sing a very light, joyful chorus to the
        bride.
     N.B. The four verses for soloists could easily be
     performed as unison choral passages. After some
     intervening dialogue, the chorus is briefly reprised.

575 1. Act III, No. 15, "Was gleicht wohl auf Erden"
     2. unison male voices; TTBB solo quartet
     3. 4.5 minutes
     4. Moderately Difficult
     5. A delightful hunting chorus.
     N.B. The solo quartet could be sung by the entire
     choir, with the unison choral part sung by a small solo
     group.

Weber, Carl Maria von. *Oberon* (1826)
Librettist: James Robertson Planché, after Wieland and
   Sotheby
Publishers: Broude Bros., G. Schirmer, Universal Edition
576 1. Act I, No. 1, "Leicht, wie Feentritt nur geht"
     2. SSAT
     3. 4 minutes
     4. Medium
     5. The fairies sing a magical chorus around the
        sleeping King.

N.B. The middle section of the excerpt is scored for a solo group, although it could be sung *tutti*.

577 1. Act II, No. 7, "Ehre sei dem mächt'gen"
2. TTBB
3. 2.5 minutes
4. Medium
5. A chorus of slaves and attendants sings in praise of the powerful Caliph.

578 1. Act II, No. 10, "Wir sind hier!"
2. SATB; Puck (S)
3. 2.5 minutes
4. Moderately Difficult
5. Puck instructs a chorus of spirits of the air, earth, water, and fire to cause a wreck of the ship carrying Reiza and Huon. The music literally sparkles.

579 1. Act II, No. 13, "Wer bleib' im korallenen Schacht"
2. SSATT
3. 4 minutes
4. Moderately Difficult
5. A tightly-knit choral ensemble of mermaids, nymphs, sylphs, fairies and elves sings a buoyant, but quiet chorus. They sing of sailing lightly over the sea.

580 1. Act III, No. 18, "Für dich hat Schönheit"
2. SSA
3. 3.5 minutes
4. Medium
5. Almansor's dancing girls attempt to cheer Reiza through song and dance.

Weill, Kurt. *Aufstieg und Fall der Stadt Mahagonny* (1930)
Librettist: Bertolt Brecht
Publishers: Broude Bros., G. Schirmer, Universal Edition
581   1. Act II, No. 16, "Wer in seinem Kober bleibt"
       2. TTBB
       3. 2.5 minutes
       4. Difficult
       5. Jim has run out of money and is being led away to
          be tied up in the forest; the men comment on
          these events in this chorus.

Wolf-Ferrari, Ermanno. *I Giojelli della Madonna* (1911)
Librettists: C. Zangarini and E. Golisciani
Publisher: G. Schirmer
582   1. Act I, "Largo! Scostatevi!"
       2. SATB divisi dbl. choir
       3. 2.5 minutes
       4. Difficult
       5. In the midst of frenetic activitiy in a Neapolitan
          square, a procession in honor of the Madonna
          approaches.

Z

Zandonai, Riccardo. *Francesca da Rimini* (1914)
Librettist: Tito Ricordi, after d'Annunzio
Publisher: Ricordi
583   1. Act I, Scene 4, "Oimè!"
       2. SSAA; Francesca (S)
       3. 2 minutes
       4. Moderately Difficult
       5. Francesca and an offstage women's chorus sing a
          lovely, lyrical chorus.

Appendix: Operas Surveyed But Not Annotated

1. Operas in *Kobbe's Complete Opera Book* With No Chorus or No Excerptable Chorus

d'Albert, Eugen. *Tiefland*

Bartók, Béla. *Duke Bluebeard's Castle*

Berg, Alban. *Lulu, Wozzeck*

Birtwistle, Harrison. *The Masque of Orpheus, Punch and Judy*

Britten, Benjamin. *Albert Herring, The Burning Fiery Furnace, Curlew River, Let's Make an Opera, Noye's Fludde, Owen Wingrave, The Prodigal Son, The Turn of the Screw*

Busoni, Ferrucio. *Arlecchino, Doktor Faust*

Cimarosa, Domenico. *Il Matrimonio Segreto*

Debussy, Claude. *Pelléas et Mélisande*

Delius, Frederick. *Koanga*

Falla, Manuel de. *El Retablo de Maese Pedro*

Giordana, Umberto. *Fedora*

Handel, George Frideric. *Rinaldo*
Henze, Heinz Werner. *Die Bassariden, Boulevard Solitude, Elegy for Young Lovers, Der junge Lord, Der Prinz von Hamburg*
Holst, Gustav. *Sávitri*
Janáček, Leoš. *The Adventures of Mr. Brouček, The Cunning Little Vixen, From the House of the Dead, Katya Kabanova, The Makropulos Affair*
Leoncavallo, Ruggiero. *Pagliacci*
Martinu, Bohuslav. *Julietta*
Mascagni, Pietro. *L'Amico Fritz*
Massenet, Jules. *Le Jongleur de Nôtre Dame, Manon, Thaïs, Werther*
Menotti, Gian Carlo. *Amahl and the Night Visitors, Amelia al Ballo, The Consul, The Medium, The Telephone*
Milhaud, Darius. *Le pauvre matelot*
Orff, Carl. *Die Kluge*
Pergolesi, Giovanni. *La serva padrona*
Poulenc, Francis. *Les Mamelles de Tirésias*
Puccini, Giacomo. *La Fanciulla del West, Gianni Schicchi, Il Tabarro*
Ravel, Maurice. *L'Heure Espagnole*
Reimann, Aribert. *Lear*
Rossini, Gioacchino. *Il Barbiere di Siviglia, Le Comte Ory, Il Turco in Italia*
Sallinen, Aulis. *Ratsumies*
Schoenberg, Arnold. *Erwartung, Von Heute auf Morgen*
Shostakovich, Dimitri. *Katerina Ismailova, The Nose*
Smetana, Bedřich. *Hubička (The Kiss)*
Strauss, Richard. *Die Aegyptische Helena, Arabella, Ariadne auf Naxos, Daphne, Elktra, Intermezzo, Der Rosenkavalier, Die Schweigsame Frau, Salome*
Stravinsky, Igor. *Mavra*
Tchaikovsky, Peter Ilitsch. *Iolanta*
Thomson, Vigil. *Four Saints in Three Acts, The Mother of Us All*
Tippett, Michael. *The Knot Garden*
Vaughan Williams, Ralph. *Riders to the Sea*

Wagner, Richard. *Das Rheingold, Siegfried, Tristan und Isolde, Die Walküre*
Walton, William. *The Bear*
Wolf-Ferrari, Ermanno. *Il Segreto di Susanna, I Quattro Rusteghi*
Zimmermann, Bernd Alois. *Die Soldaten*

2. Operas in *Kobbe's Complete Opera Book* Not Available for Examination.

Adam, Adolphe. *Le Postillon de Longjumeau*
Glass, Philip. *Akhnaten*
Janáček, Leoš. *Osud*
Knussen, Oliver. *Where the Wild Things Are*
Ligeti, Györgi. *Le Grande Macabre*
Ullmann, Viktor. *Der Kaiser von Atlantis*

3. Works listed in *Kobbé's Complete Opera Book* Not Considered to be Operas

Handel, George Frideric. *Semele*
Monteverdi, Claudio. *Arianna, Il Combattimento di Tancredi e Clorinda*
Poulenc, Francis. *La Voix Humaine*

Index to Titles of Operas

Index to First Lines
and Titles of Scenes

Index to Librettists

Index to Choral
Performing Forces

WOMEN'S VOICES ONLY

UNISON VOICES
Boito, 75 (boys)
Britten, 75 (men), 98-99
   (women), 100 (mixed)
Tchaikovsky, 443 (men)
Weber, 575 (men)

Index to Difficulty
Level of Excerpts

Index to Duration
of Excerpts

About the Authors

DAVID P. DEVENNEY (B.M., Iowa State University; M.M., University of Wisconsin-Madison; D.M.A., University of Cincinnati) is Associate Professor of Music and Director of Humanities Programs at Otterbein College; he previously taught on the faculty of Virginia Polytechnic Institute and State University. At Otterbein, he conducts the Chorale and the Early Music Ensemble, and teaches courses in music history and conducting. He is also Music Director of VocalBaroque, a professional-calibre early music ensemble in Columbus, Ohio. Besides his many choral performances, Dr. DeVenney is the author of a four-volume reference series on American choral music, as well as a wide range of articles dealing with various topics in choral music.

CRAIG R. JOHNSON (B.M., M.M., Northwestern University; D.M.A., University of Cincinnati) is Associate Professor of Music and Director of Choral and Vocal Activities at Otterbein College. His responsibilities at Otterbein include conducting the Concert Choir and Opus One, a vocal jazz ensemble, in addition to teaching classes in music theory, conducting, and voice. Dr. Johnson also serves as musical/stage director for the Otterbein opera theatre program, and is active as an adjudicator, clinician, and baritone soloist.